Sentencing Sex Offenders

Affirmative Action	Media Bias
Amateur Athletics	Mental Health Reform
American Military Policy	Miranda Rights
Animal Rights	Open Government
Bankruptcy Law	Physician-Assisted Suicide
Blogging	Policing the Internet
Capital Punishment, Second Edition	Prescription and Non-prescription Drugs
Disaster Relief	Prisoners' Rights
DNA Evidence	Private Property Rights
Drugs and Sports	Protecting Ideas
Educational Standards	Religion in Public Schools
Election Reform	Rights of Students
The FCC and Regulating Indecency	The Right to Die
	The Right to Privacy
Fetal Rights	Search and Seizure
Food Safety	Sentencing Sex Offenders
Freedom of Speech	Smoking Bans, Second Edition
Gay Rights	Stem Cell Research and Cloning
Gun Control	Tort Reform
Immigrants' Rights After 9/11	Trial of Juveniles as Adults
Immigration Policy	The War on Terror, Second Edition
Legalized Gambling	
Legalizing Marijuana	Welfare Reform
Mandatory Military Service	Women in the Military

Sentencing Sex Offenders

David L. Hudson Jr.

SERIES CONSULTING EDITOR
Alan Marzilli, M.A., J.D.

An imprint of Infobase Publishing

Sentencing Sex Offenders

Copyright © 2009 by Infobase Publishing

All rights reserved. No part of this book may be reproduced or utilized in any form or by any means, electronic or mechanical, including photocopying, recording, or by any information storage or retrieval systems, without permission in writing from the publisher. For information, contact:

Chelsea House
An imprint of Infobase Publishing
132 West 31st Street
New York NY 10001

Library of Congress Cataloging-in-Publication Data

Hudson, David L., 1969–
  Sentencing sex offenders / David L. Hudson Jr.
    p. cm. — (Point/counterpoint)
  Includes bibliographical references and index.
  ISBN 978-1-60413-079-9 (hardcover)
  1. Sentences (Criminal procedure)—United States. 2. Sex offenders—United States. I. Title. II. Series.
  KF9685.H83 2008
  345.73'0253—dc22   2008027123

Chelsea House books are available at special discounts when purchased in bulk quantities for businesses, associations, institutions, or sales promotions. Please call our Special Sales Department in New York at (212) 967-8800 or (800) 322-8755.

You can find Chelsea House on the World Wide Web at
http://www.chelseahouse.com

Series design by Keith Trego
Cover design by Keith Trego and Ben Peterson

Printed in the United States of America

Bang NMSG 10 9 8 7 6 5 4 3 2 1

This book is printed on acid-free paper.

All links and Web addresses were checked and verified to be correct at the time of publication. Because of the dynamic nature of the Web, some addresses and links may have changed since publication and may no longer be valid.

POINT COUNTERPOINT

Foreword	**6**
INTRODUCTION The Sex Offender Problem	**10**
POINT Registration and Notification Requirements for Convicted Sex Offenders Are Constitutional	**21**
COUNTERPOINT Registration and Notification Laws Are Unconstitutional	**31**
POINT Residency Restrictions Are a Constitutional Way to Protect Victims from Sex Offenders	**39**
COUNTERPOINT Residency Restrictions Against Sexual Offenders Violate Constitutional Rights	**48**
POINT Civil Commitment of Violent Sexual Predators Is Necessary and Constitutional	**56**
COUNTERPOINT Civil Commitment Proceedings Are Punitive and Violate Constitutional Rights	**65**
CONCLUSION Unanswered Questions and the Future of Sex Offender Legislation	**74**
Appendix: Beginning Legal Research	79
Elements of the Argument	82
Notes	84
Resources	87
Picture Credits	90
Index	91

FOREWORD

**Alan Marzilli, M.A., J.D.
Birmingham, Alabama**

The POINT/COUNTERPOINT series offers the reader a greater understanding of some of the most controversial issues in contemporary American society—issues such as capital punishment, immigration, gay rights, and gun control. We have looked for the most contemporary issues and have included topics—such as the controversies surrounding "blogging"—that we could not have imagined when the series began.

In each volume, the author has selected an issue of particular importance and set out some of the key arguments on both sides of the issue. Why study both sides of the debate? Maybe you have yet to make up your mind on an issue, and the arguments presented in the book will help you to form an opinion. More likely, however, you will already have an opinion on many of the issues covered by the series. There is always the chance that you will change your opinion after reading the arguments for the other side. But even if you are firmly committed to an issue—for example, school prayer or animal rights—reading both sides of the argument will help you to become a more effective advocate for your cause. By gaining an understanding of opposing arguments, you can develop answers to those arguments.

Perhaps more importantly, listening to the other side sometimes helps you see your opponent's arguments in a more human way. For example, Sister Helen Prejean, one of the nation's most visible opponents of capital punishment, has been deeply affected by her interactions with the families of murder victims. By seeing the families' grief and pain, she understands much better why people support the death penalty, and she is able to carry out her advocacy with a greater sensitivity to the needs and beliefs of death penalty supporters.

The books in the series include numerous features that help the reader to gain a greater understanding of the issues. Real-life examples illustrate the human side of the issues. Each chapter also includes excerpts from relevant laws, court cases, and other material, which provide a better foundation for understanding the arguments. The volumes contain citations to relevant sources of law and information, and an appendix guides the reader through the basics of legal research, both on the Internet and in the library. Today, through free Web sites, it is easy to access legal documents, and these books might give you ideas for your own research.

Studying the issues covered by the Point/Counterpoint series is more than an academic activity. The issues described in the book affect all of us as citizens. They are the issues that today's leaders debate and tomorrow's leaders will decide. While all of the issues covered in the Point/Counterpoint series are controversial today, and will remain so for the foreseeable future, it is entirely possible that the reader might one day play a central role in resolving the debate. Today it might seem that some debates—such as capital punishment and abortion—will never be resolved.

However, our nation's history is full of debates that seemed as though they never would be resolved, and many of the issues are now well settled—at least on the surface. In the nineteenth century, abolitionists met with widespread resistance to their efforts to end slavery. Ultimately, the controversy threatened the union, leading to the Civil War between the northern and southern states. Today, while a public debate over the merits of slavery would be unthinkable, racism persists in many aspects of society.

Similarly, today nobody questions women's right to vote. Yet at the beginning of the twentieth century, suffragists fought public battles for women's voting rights, and it was not until the passage of the Nineteenth Amendment in 1920 that the legal right of women to vote was established nationwide.

What makes an issue controversial? Often, controversies arise when most people agree that there is a problem, but people disagree about the best way to solve the problem. There is little argument that poverty is a major problem in the United States, especially in inner cities and rural areas. Yet, people disagree vehemently about the best way to address the problem. To some, the answer is social programs, such as welfare, food stamps, and public housing. However, many argue that such subsidies encourage dependence on government benefits while unfairly penalizing those who work and pay taxes, and that the real solution is to require people to support themselves.

American society is in a constant state of change, and sometimes modern practices clash with what many consider to be "traditional values," which are often rooted in conservative political views or religious beliefs. Many blame high crime rates, and problems such as poverty, illiteracy, and drug use on the breakdown of the traditional family structure of a married mother and father raising their children. Since the "sexual revolution" of the 1960s and 1970s, sparked in part by the widespread availability of the birth control pill, marriage rates have declined, and the number of children born outside of marriage has increased. The sexual revolution led to controversies over birth control, sex education, and other issues, most prominently abortion. Similarly, the gay rights movement has been challenged as a threat to traditional values. While many gay men and lesbians want to have the same right to marry and raise families as heterosexuals, many politicians and others have challenged gay marriage and adoption as a threat to American society.

Sometimes, new technology raises issues that we have never faced before, and society disagrees about the best solution. Are people free to swap music online, or does this violate the copyright laws that protect songwriters and musicians' ownership of the music that they create? Should scientists use "genetic engineering" to create new crops that are resistant to disease and pests and produce more food, or is it too risky to use a laboratory to create plants that nature never intended? Modern medicine has continued to increase the average lifespan—which is now 77 years, up from under 50 years at the beginning of the twentieth century—but many people are now choosing to die in comfort rather than living with painful ailments in their later years. For doctors, this presents an ethical dilemma: should they allow their patients to die? Should they assist patients in ending their own lives painlessly?

Perhaps the most controversial issues are those that implicate a constitutional right. The Bill of Rights—the first 10 amendments to the U.S. Constitution—spell out some of the most fundamental rights that distinguish our democracy from other nations with fewer freedoms. However, the sparsely-worded document is open to interpretation, with each side saying that the Constitution is on their side. The Bill of Rights was meant to protect individual liberties; however, the needs of some individuals clash with society's needs. Thus, the Constitution often serves as a battleground between individuals and government officials seeking to protect society in some way. The First Amendment's guarantee of "freedom of speech" leads to some very difficult questions. Some forms of expression—such as burning an American flag—lead to public outrage, but are protected by the First Amendment. Other types of expression that most people find objectionable—such as child pornography—are not protected by the Constitution. The question is not only where to draw the line, but whether drawing lines around constitutional rights threatens our liberty.

The Bill of Rights raises many other questions about individual rights and societal "good." Is a prayer before a high school football game an "establishment of religion" prohibited by the First Amendment? Does the Second Amendment's promise of "the right to bear arms" include concealed handguns? Does stopping and frisking someone standing on a known drug corner constitute "unreasonable search and seizure" in violation of the Fourth Amendment? Although the U.S. Supreme Court has the ultimate authority in interpreting the U.S. Constitution, their answers do not always satisfy the public. When a group of nine people—sometimes by a five-to-four vote—makes a decision that affects hundreds of millions of others, public outcry can be expected. For example, the Supreme Court's 1973 ruling in *Roe v. Wade* that abortion is protected by the Constitution did little to quell the debate over abortion.

Whatever the root of the controversy, the books in the POINT/COUNTERPOINT series seek to explain to the reader both the origins of the debate, the current state of the law, and the arguments on either side of the debate. Our hope in creating this series is that the reader will be better informed about the issues facing not only our politicians, but all of our nation's citizens, and become more actively involved in resolving these debates, as voters, concerned citizens, journalists, or maybe even elected officials.

INTRODUCTION

The Sex Offender Problem

In recent years, there has been acute popular and official concern with managing those perceived to be a danger to society. Pedophiles in particular have captured the public imagination and have become in a sense the new "moral panic."[1]

—Anne-Marie McAlinden, *The Shaming of Sexual Offenders: Risk, Retribution and Reintegration*, 2007

One of the most pressing social, moral, and legal dilemmas of recent times has been what to do with those who commit predatory acts of sexual violence. The U.S. Supreme Court said it bluntly in 2002: "Sex offenders are a serious threat in this Nation."[2] One option is to impose greater criminal sentences on those who are found guilty of serious sexual crimes including rape, sexual battery, sexual assault, child molestation, and solicitation of a minor. This is reflected in several state laws known as "Jessica's Laws," which call for a minimum sentence of 25 years for sexual crimes.

An even greater problem occurs when a convicted sex offender fulfills his criminal sentence and, presumably, has paid his debt to society. The question now becomes what post-incarceration sanctions can be imposed on such individuals. This problem arises because some sex offenders attack again. Many argue that sex offenders have an especially high rate of *recidivism*, meaning that they commit another similar crime after committing a first one (or several). There have been highly reported instances in which a young child was raped and/or murdered by a previously convicted sex offender. Society, then, is right to ask what can be done to protect minors and others from individuals who may be predisposed to commit such crimes, and those who have committed such crimes in the past.

A series of high-profile cases has led to a series of federal and state laws designed to regulate such sex offenders. The first type of sex offender law concerns so-called registration and notification laws. These laws require convicted sex offenders to register with law enforcement officials, providing their current name, address, place of employment, and other personal information. In conjunction with registration, many laws require the public to be notified that a sex offender is moving into their neighborhood. Sometimes, these notification provisions include the posting of information about sex offenders on an online registry that allows anyone to search for sex offenders by name or zip code. For example, Tennessee has its Tennessee Sexual Offender Registry,[3] on which one can search for sex offenders by name, city, county, or zip code. The registry then provides viewers with a host of information, including name, date of birth, current address, classification of offender, and convicted offense.

The movement for sexual offender registration and notification laws in part came from the case of eight-year-old Jacob Erwin Wetterling. In October 1989, eight-year-old Jacob, his brother, and a friend rode their bicycles from a local convenience store in their hometown of St. Joseph, Missouri. As the three boys were biking, a masked man with a gun appeared and ordered the boys to drop their bikes and lay facedown on the ground. The abductor allowed Jacob's brother and the friend to run away, but kept Jacob. To this day, Jacob's and the abductor's whereabouts are unknown.

This crime led to the federal congressional passage in 1994 of the Jacob Wetterling Crimes Against Children Sex Offender Registration Act, or Jacob's Law. This law required states to pass laws creating registries of sexually violent predators. The law did not, however, require state officials to release information about these predators to the public. Some states decided not to provide public notification.

That changed after another child abduction involving a seven-year-old girl named Megan Nicole Kanka, who lived with her parents in Hamilton Township, New Jersey. Kanka's parents were unaware that convicted sex offenders lived right across the street. One of them was Jesse Timmendequas, who lived in a house with several other men, two of whom also had been convicted of prior sex offenses.

Timmendequas had a dangerous history. In 1979, he confessed to the attempted abduction of a five-year-old girl in

THE LETTER OF THE LAW

Sexually violent predator: "a person who has been convicted of a sexually violent offense and who suffers from a mental abnormality or personality disorder that makes the person likely to engage in predatory sexually violent offenses."

Source: 42 U.S.C. § 14071(a)(3)(C)_

Piscataway, New Jersey. He initially received a suspended sentence upon the condition of undergoing treatment, but he refused treatment and was sentenced to nine months in jail. After his release, he later was charged with sexually assaulting another young girl, this time in Aventel, New Jersey. He served six years in prison for that offense.[4]

Timmendequas later confessed to sexually abusing and killing Megan Kanka. He was sentenced to death, but years later his sentence was changed to life in prison. Megan's parents made it their life's mission to provide more information to parents about former sex offenders in society. The result was a so-called "Megan's Law" in New Jersey. In 1996, Congress amended the

THE LETTER OF THE LAW

Federal Version of Megan's Law

SECTION 1.
This Act may be cited as "Megan's Law".

SEC. 2. RELEASE OF INFORMATION AND CLARIFICATION OF PUBLIC NATURE OF INFORMATION.
Section 170101 (d) of the Violent Crime Control and Law Enforcement Act of 1994 (42 U.S.C. 14071 (d)) is amended to read as follows:

(d) Release of Information—
  (1) The information collected under a State registration Program may be disclosed for any purpose permitted under the laws of the State.
  (2) The designated State law enforcement agency and any local law enforcement agency authorized by the State agency shall release relevant information that is necessary to protect the public concerning a specific person required to register under this section, except that the identity of a victim of an offense that requires registration under this section shall not be released.

Source: Public Law 104–105, available online at http://www.megannicolekankafoundation.org/federal_law.htm.

Officer H.C. Davis of the Virginia State Police demonstrates upgrades to the Virginia Sex Offender registry in 2006. Among the upgrades was a map that can pinpoint the locations of convicted sex offenders. More and more such registries have capabilities like this, many of which can be accessed by the public.

Jacob Wetterling Act with the federal Megan's Law. This amendment required states to release information to the public about former sex offenders in their communities.

As a result of Megan's Law, most states began providing online registries that enable anyone to type in information and find out the location of former sex offenders. Still, even after Megan's Law, it was determined that more information was needed since some states did not provide detailed information.

Enter "Adam's Law." In July 1981, a young boy named Adam Walsh was abducted from a mall in Hollywood, Florida, and murdered. Two weeks later, Adam's remains were discovered in a canal more than 100 miles from his home. His crime was never solved, and his parents, John and Reve, dedicated their lives to the protection of children. In 2006, Congress passed the Adam Walsh Child Protection and Safety Act of 2006. This new law creates three tiers, or classifications, of sex offenders and establishes a national registration program of sex offenders. Adam's Law also made it mandatory for states to maintain an online registry about sex offenders that can be accessed by the public. It requires sex offenders to register within three days after they move to a new state.

Much of the legislation regarding sex offenders first happens at the state level. Another tragic incident that prompted state legislation occurred in Florida when convicted sex offender John Couey raped and murdered nine-year-old Jessica Lunsford. That caused the state of Florida to pass what is known as "Jessica's Law." More than 40 states have passed their own version of Jessica's Law. Key features of these laws include greater

Legal Language

a) In General.—Except as provided in this section, each jurisdiction shall make available on the Internet, in a manner that is readily accessible to all jurisdictions and to the public, all information about each sex offender in the registry. The jurisdiction shall maintain the Internet site in a manner that will permit the public to obtain relevant information for each sex offender by a single query for any given zip code or geographic radius set by the user. The jurisdiction shall also include in the design of its Internet site all field search capabilities needed for full participation in the Dru Sjodin National Sex Offender Public Web site and shall participate in that website as provided by the Attorney General.

Source: 18 U.S.C. §16918

mandatory minimum sentences for sex offenders and electronic monitoring of certain child sexual predators for life when they are released from prison.

Residency Restrictions

Community registration and notification laws receive arguably the bulk of the press regarding sex offender legislation. In addition to that, however, more and more communities are responding with their own regulations that not only require sex offenders to register, but also regulate where they can live. These are often called residency restrictions. Some of these laws

President George W. Bush on Signing the Adam Walsh Legislation

Protecting our children is our solemn responsibility. It's what we must do. When a child's life or innocence is taken, it is a terrible loss—it's an act of unforgivable cruelty. Our society has a duty to protect our children from exploitation and danger. By enacting this law, we're sending a clear message across the country: Those who prey on our children will be caught, prosecuted, and punished to the fullest extent of the law....

This new law I sign today builds on the progress in four important ways: First, the bill I sign today will greatly expand the National Sex Offender Registry by integrating the information in state sex offender registry systems and ensuring that law enforcement has access to the same information across the United States. It seems to make sense, doesn't it? See, these improvements will help prevent sex offenders from evading detection by moving from one state to the next. Data drawn from this comprehensive registry will also be made available to the public so parents have the information they need to protect their children from sex offenders that might be in their neighborhoods.

Second, the bill I sign today will increase federal penalties for crimes against children. This bill imposes tough mandatory minimum penalties for the most serious crimes against our children. It increases penalties for crimes such as sex trafficking of children and child prostitution; provides grants to states to help them prohibit sex offenders from living within a certain distance from a school, park, youth program center, or any place likely to be frequented by minors. Another common feature of such laws prohibits a convicted sex offender from living within a certain distance of his previous victim.

Proponents argue that such laws are a valid way to control the location of dangerous sex offenders. The rationale is that, if sex offenders are not around children, they are less likely or less able to attack again. Also, these laws make the community feel safer. Opponents counter that these laws are a classic form of banishment and simply go too far. For example, an Indiana

---

institutionalize sex offenders who've shown they cannot change their behavior and are about to be released from prison.

Third, the bill I sign today will make it harder for sex predators to reach our children on the Internet. Some sex predators use this technology to make contact with potential victims, so the bill authorizes additional new regional Internet Crimes Against Children Task Forces. These task forces provide funding and training to help state and local law enforcement combat crimes involving the sexual exploitation of minors on the Internet.

Fourth, the bill I sign today will help prevent child abuse by creating a National Child Abuse Registry, and requiring investigators to do background checks on adoptive and foster parents before they approve to take custody of a child. By giving child protective service professionals in all 50 states access to this critical information, we will improve their ability to investigate child abuse cases and help ensure that the vulnerable children are not put into situations of abuse or neglect.

This is a comprehensive piece of legislation, and it's an important bill. Our nation grieves with every family that's suffered the unbearable pain of a child who's been abducted or abused. This law makes an important step forward in this country's efforts to protect those who cannot protect themselves.

Source: White House Press Release, "President Signs H.R. 4472, the Adam Walsh Child Protection and Safety Act of 2006," July 27, 2006, available online at http://www.whitehouse.gov/news/releases/2006/07/20060727-6.html.

appeals court in May 2008 invalidated a residency restriction that prohibited a convicted sex offender from living in a home that he had owned for more than 20 years.[5]

Civil Commitment Laws

About 20 states have passed an even more restrictive measure on convicted sex offenders: civil commitment or civil confinement laws. These measures allow the state to keep a convicted sex offender "civilly confined" in a state institution, even after the offender has completed his criminal sentence. The argument is that there are certain sexually violent predators who are so likely to attack again that society must be protected from them.

Proponents argue for victim protection. If an individual truly is a sexually violent predator and has been found to be very likely to commit another crime, it is incumbent upon society to provide the necessary protection. If a child molester admits he is going to molest another child, or it is proven that he is going to do so, the state has a moral responsibility to protect its populace. Supporters also point out that there is a long history of civil confinement of certain mentally ill and mentally challenged individuals who are shown to be a danger to society.

Opponents counter that these measures are not "civil," but rather punitive, criminal measures that seek to add on to a person's criminal sentence. Traditionally, once a person completes his prison sentence, he has paid his debt to society. It violates basic notions of fairness and constitutional principles to impose a second punishment on an individual for the same offense.

This book examines the controversy over the regulation of sex offenders through the prism of these three types of sex offender laws: registration and notification laws, residency restrictions, and civil commitment laws. It is hoped that both proponents and opponents of such measures will gain insight into the arguments from the other side. No one questions the compelling governmental interest in protecting children from harm. The question is whether these laws unfairly trample on the rights of sex offenders, particularly those who have paid their debt to society by completing their prison sentences. Some argue that more time should be spent on treating sex offenders, rather than shaming them with various forms of "Scarlet Letters" upon their release from prison. There are no easy answers to this difficult dilemma.

Registration and Notification Requirements for Convicted Sex Offenders Are Constitutional

Richard and Maureen Kanka lived in a seemingly peaceful neighborhood in Hamilton Township, New Jersey, with their young daughter, Megan. By all accounts, it appeared to be an idyllic place to raise a young child. Then, Megan disappeared one day after riding her bike. The Kankas were shocked, and the community helped them in trying to locate their missing daughter. Unfortunately, it turned out to be every parent's worst nightmare, as former convicted sex offender Jesse Timmendequas confessed to raping and murdering Megan. Timmendequas lived across the street from the Kankas, who had no idea that this bespectacled man was a convicted sex offender—a man who had served years in prison for sexually violent offenses involving children. "We knew nothing about him," Maureen Kanka said. "If we had been aware of his record, my daughter would be alive today."[6]

The Kankas began to devote their lives to ensuring that other parents would receive notification when a sex offender moved near their home. "Every parent should have the right to know if a dangerous sexual predator moves into their neighborhood," the Kankas said.[7] The Kankas circulated a petition that soon had more than 400,000 signatures. The New Jersey legislature received the message and acted quickly, passing "Megan's Law."

The momentum did not stop with New Jersey. Every state has a Megan's Law that imposes registration and notification requirements on convicted sex offenders. Congress took notice as well and in 1996 unanimously passed amendments to Jacob's Law with a "federal Megan's Law." The vote was unanimous, and President Bill Clinton signed the legislation into law on May 17, 1996. The law provided that "information collected under a State registration Program may be disclosed for any purpose permitted under the laws of the State." The law also provided:

> The designated State law enforcement agency and any local law enforcement agency authorized by the State agency shall release relevant information that is necessary to protect the public concerning a specific person required to register under this section, except that the identity of a victim of an offense that requires registration under this section shall not be released.[8]

The movement to provide better tools for parents continued with the Adam Walsh Act, described in the introduction of this book. The Adam Walsh Act expands on Jacob's Law and Megan's Law by creating a National Child Abuse Registry that increases the public's knowledge about child predators.

The various state Megan's Laws are designed to inform parents, protect children, and prevent the future abuse of children. Some reports have indicated that 1 in 5 girls will be sexually

Registration and Notification Requirements Are Constitutional

exploited before reaching adulthood and 1 in 10 boys will suffer a similar fate. That is too many. Megan's Law is not a cure-all, but it can be an important tool in helping to reduce the horrors of child abuse and other sexual offenses.

Megan's Laws are constitutional and do not violate the rights of convicted sex offenders.

Some complain that Megan's Laws violate the constitutional rights of convicted sex offenders. They argue that those offenders who serve their sentences have paid their debt to society and should not be burdened with registration and notification requirements that could lead to vigilantism, harassment, and other problems for them.

The reality is that no less an authority than the U.S. Supreme Court has rejected constitutional challenges to state Megan's Laws. The court upheld the constitutionality of two sex offender registration laws from Alaska and Connecticut in *Smith v. Doe* (2003)[9] and *Connecticut Department of Public Safety v. Doe* (2003).[10]

The Alaska law required sex offenders to register with the state within 30 days after their release. If the offender was convicted of an aggravated offense or multiple offenses, he or she had to register for life. The information was forwarded to a department of public safety that maintained a central registry of sex offenders. Much of the information is then made public, including the sex offender's name, aliases, address, photograph, physical description, license numbers of vehicles, place of employment, date of birth, crime, length of sentence, and a statement as to whether the person is currently complying with the law. The law applied retroactively even to individuals who had completed their criminal sentences before the passage of the law.

Two sex offenders challenged the Alaska law anonymously. They had completed their sentences and undergone rehabilitation programs before the passage of the law. They argued that

The family of Megan Kanka, whose 1994 death provided the inspiration for Megan's Law, watches as acting New Jersey governor Donald T. DiFranceso signs a bill that created an Internet registry of New Jersey sex offenders.

Alaska's registration and notification requirements violated due process and the ex post facto clause of the U.S. Constitution. An ex post facto law is a retroactive law that alters the legal status of a person, imposing new legal obligations on him or her after the fact.

The U.S. Supreme Court rejected the offenders' constitutional arguments and determined that the law was a civil and not a punitive one. The men had argued that posting information to the public about their past criminal conviction amounted to a modern-day Scarlet Letter and was akin to banishment or expulsion, older punishments that are considered out of touch with modern society. The Supreme Court rejected that analogy, writing: "The stigma of Alaska's Megan's Law results not from public display for ridicule and shaming but from the dissemination

Registration and Notification Requirements Are Constitutional

of accurate information about a public record, most of which is already public."[11]

Connecticut had its own Megan's Laws that provided for a central database of sex offenders that could be accessed by the public on the Internet. A convicted sex offender who completed his sentence sued, claiming that his due-process rights were violated because he was not a sex offender who posed any sort of future threat to the public. He argued that the statute was flawed because it lumped all sex offenders together and placed them up for public shaming.

The U.S. Supreme Court rejected those arguments, writing that the fact that the plaintiff may not be a danger is "of no consequence."[12] The Court also pointed out that on the sex offender registry there was a disclaimer stating that "individuals included

FROM THE BENCH

Justice Anthony Kennedy in *Smith v. Doe*

Although the public availability of the information may have a lasting and painful impact on the convicted sex offender, these consequences flow not from the Act's registration and dissemination provisions, but from the fact of conviction, already a matter of public record. The State makes the facts underlying the offenses and the resulting convictions accessible so members of the public can take the precautions they deem necessary before dealing with the registrant....

Alaska could conclude that a conviction for a sex offense provides evidence of substantial risk of recidivism. The legislature's findings are consistent with grave concerns over the high rate of recidivism among convicted sex offenders and their dangerousness as a class. The risk of recidivism posed by sex offenders is frightening and high....

Our examination of the Act's effects leads to the determination that respondents cannot show, much less by the clearest proof, that the effects of the law negate Alaska's intention to establish a civil regulatory scheme. The Act is nonpunitive and its retroactive application does not violate the Ex Post Facto Clause.

Source: *Smith v. Doe*, 538 U.S. 84 (2003).

within the registry are included *solely* by virtue of their conviction record and state law."[13]

State courts have also upheld Megan's Law from a variety of constitutional challenges. The Supreme Court of Illinois ruled that its state law was valid in *People v. Cornelius*.[14] The case involved a convicted sex offender who had failed to properly comply with the state's sex offender registration law because he did not notify authorities that he had changed addresses.

The defendant also argued that other provisions of the law were unconstitutional, including the provisions that made his personal information—such as his name, address, and photograph—available on the Internet for anyone to access. Before the Illinois law

THE LETTER OF THE LAW

Illinois Sex Offender Registration Law

§ 730 ILCS 150/3. Duty to register
(a) A sex offender, as defined in Section 2 of this Act, or sexual predator shall, within the time period prescribed in subsections (b) and (c), register in person and provide accurate information as required by the Department of State Police. Such information shall include a current photograph, current address, current place of employment, the employer's telephone number, school attended, all e-mail addresses, instant messaging identities, chat room identities, and other Internet communications identities that the sex offender uses or plans to use, all Uniform Resource Locators (URLs) registered or used by the sex offender, all blogs and other Internet sites maintained by the sex offender or to which the sex offender has uploaded any content or posted any messages or information, extensions of the time period for registering as provided in this Article and, if an extension was granted, the reason why the extension was granted and the date the sex offender was notified of the extension. The information shall also include the county of conviction, license plate numbers for every vehicle registered in the name of the sex offender, the age of the sex offender at the time of the commission of the offense, the age of the victim at the time of the commission of the offense, and any distinguishing marks located on the body of the sex offender. A sex offender convicted under Section 11–6, 11–20.1, 11–20.3, or 11–21 of the Criminal Code of 1961 shall

Registration and Notification Requirements Are Constitutional

made these details available on the Internet, a person had to go to the state police to request information about a specific sex offender. The Illinois Supreme Court rejected the privacy argument, writing: "We agree with the State that the Internet access to sex offender registry information authorized [under state law] . . . is simply another manner of archiving, storing, and disseminating the information already available by numerous other means-to-interested parties."[15]

The Illinois court explained that "the determinative fact is that sex offender registry information is already open to the public and is a matter of public record" and that "the Internet provides for a different kind of accessibility to information that is already publicly available by other means."[16]

---

provide all Internet protocol (IP) addresses in his or her residence, registered in his or her name, accessible at his or her place of employment, or otherwise under his or her control or custody. The sex offender or sexual predator shall register:

(1) with the chief of police in the municipality in which he or she resides or is temporarily domiciled for a period of time of 5 or more days, unless the municipality is the City of Chicago, in which case he or she shall register at the Chicago Police Department Headquarters; or

(2) with the sheriff in the county in which he or she resides or is temporarily domiciled for a period of time of 5 or more days in an unincorporated area or, if incorporated, no police chief exists.

If the sex offender or sexual predator is employed at or attends an institution of higher education, he or she shall register:

(i) with the chief of police in the municipality in which he or she is employed at or attends an institution of higher education, unless the municipality is the City of Chicago, in which case he or she shall register at the Chicago Police Department Headquarters; or

(ii) with the sheriff in the county in which he or she is employed or attends an institution of higher education located in an unincorporated area, or if incorporated, no police chief exists.

Megan's Laws help communities to become safer while denouncing sex offenses.

Perhaps the best argument for Megan's Laws is that such laws have had the effect of reducing sexual abuse of children. The

FROM THE BENCH

Illinois Supreme Court Points to Alaska's Precedent in Upholding Its Own Sex Offender Registration Law

It must be acknowledged that notice of a criminal conviction subjects the offender to public shame, the humiliation increasing in proportion to the extent of the publicity. And the geographic reach of the Internet is greater than anything that could have been designed in colonial times. These facts do not render Internet notification punitive. The purpose and the principal effect of notification are to inform the public for its own safety, not to humiliate the offender. Widespread public access is necessary for the efficacy of the scheme, and the attendant humiliation is but a collateral consequence of a valid regulation.

The State's Web site does not provide the public with means to shame the offender by, say, posting comments underneath his record. An individual seeking the information must take the initial step of going to the Department of Public Safety's Web site, proceed to the sex offender registry, and then look up the desired information. The process is more analogous to a visit than to a scheme forcing an offender to appear in public with some visible badge of past criminality. The Internet makes the document search more efficient, cost effective, and convenient for Alaska's citizenry.

Thus, informed by the analysis of the Supreme Court in *Smith*, we conclude that Illinois may permissibly use the Internet dissemination of sex offender registry information as a more efficient, cost effective, and convenient means of providing its citizens with important public information.... The collateral effects flowing from the dissemination of sex offender information are substantially outweighed by the goal of safeguarding the public—especially children—from convicted sex offenders.

Source: *People v. Cornelius*, 213 Ill. 2nd 178 (Ill. 2004)

Crimes Against Children Research Center reports that there has been a dramatic drop in cases, more than 50 percent since 1992. Between 2005 and 2006 alone, child sex abuse cases dropped 5 percent.[17]

Megan's Laws help communities to become safer, or at least to feel safer, by denouncing abhorrent behavior that the community will not tolerate. Legal commentator Brian J. Telpner argues that "community notification sends a clear signal that law-abiding society simply will not tolerate certain community sex crimes, particularly those against minors."[18]

Views of Legal Commentator Brian J. Telpner

That Megan's Laws enable communities to construct themselves as "safe" is demonstrated by the complacency communities feel after enacting such laws. Some have noted that, despite the practical shortcomings of these laws, knowing where a sexual predator lives, and publicizing it, may help to soothe a nation frustrated by child murders. These laws reflect a deep need for such profound risks to be identified and labeled, which in turn fosters feelings of security and insulation....

In the final analysis, community notification provisions are more about the communities that promulgate such laws than the offenders who are their targets. More than simply revealing identities of convicted child sex offenders living in our communities, Megan's Laws enable non-sex offenders to build communities based on the belief that they are free from the burden of ferreting out these undesirable and dangerous elements. That such laws are needed testifies to the dissolution of the concept of community in our mobile and heterogeneous modern age. Even though we know such laws do not often prevent convicted child sex offenders from striking again, community notification provisions soothe our psyches by facilitating our efforts to view our communities, our children, and our ourselves as secure.

Source: Brian J. Telpner, "Constructing Safe Communities: Megan's Laws and the Purposes of Punishment," *Georgetown Law Journal* 85 (1997): 2039-2068 at p. 2042, 2068.

Summary

Law enforcement officials have a duty to protect the public. Sex offenders are a peculiar class of offenders who are likely to commit their crimes again. Megan Kanka was killed by a repeat sex offender; so was Jessica Lunsford, and so were countless other victims. If Megan's parents and the parents of other children had known a convicted sex offender lived near them, they may have been able to save their children's lives.

Yes, registration and notification requirements place additional burdens on the lives of convicted sex offenders; but these individuals deserve those additional burdens because the greater good involves the protection of children and other potential victims. The U.S. Supreme Court has upheld two Megan's Laws from the states of Alaska and Connecticut. The court rejected constitutional challenges by anonymous sex offenders.

The fact is, however, that these offenders' criminal cases are public record. Their criminal convictions are truthful information. How could the release of important, truthful information designed to protect minors be found unconstitutional? The answer is that it cannot.

COUNTERPOINT

Registration and Notification Laws Are Unconstitutional

Two men in Phillipsburg, New Jersey, knew that a recently paroled sex offender lived in the area. They knew this because of notification requirements in their state's Megan's Law. Wearing black ski masks, the two men knocked down the door of the supposed sex offender's home at around three in the morning, demanding, "Where is the child molester?" The two intruders then began beating a man they thought was the sex offender, but who turned out to be the wrong man.[19] "This is exactly the concern that we had when the law was being considered for passage, that it would be used to enable vigilantism rather than for any legitimate community interest," said the legal director of the American Civil Liberties Union in New Jersey.[20]

In Linden, New Jersey, a paroled child rapist awoke from a deep sleep after gunfire tore through his windows. A 23-year-old man later admitted to firing into the home after learning that the convicted sex offender was moving into the neighborhood. "I'm out of prison," the sex offender told the *New York Times*. "But it's like I'm in the big prison now.... I'm the victim here. My whole neighborhood is, too, and so is my family."[21]

Another sex offender had a similar experience. This man had served a collective total of 42 years in prison for killing a boy when he was 14 and then sodomizing another when he was in his forties. He was due for parole at 62 years old, and thought he could live with his sister, who had offered to allow him to live with her. Then, community notification took place under Megan's Law. Many neighbors voiced their objections to him living in their neighborhood, and some closely watched the sister's house. The community pressure became intense enough that she took back the offer to her brother. Having nowhere to go, he had to stay in prison. This case "calls into question the results of new laws intended to force authorities to tell neighbors in advance,

QUOTABLE

Howard University law professor Rachel King

At the time of their inception, many civil libertarians opposed sex offender registries, believing that they violated the privacy of the offender and fearing that the registries would encourage vigilantism. Those fears were warranted. Every year, there are numerous crimes, including murder, against convicted sex offenders who comply with registration laws. At the same time, the government has not undertaken any research to establish if the laws succeed in making communities safer. Besides risking vigilantism, sex offender laws often make it difficult for people to rehabilitate themselves by making it more difficult for offenders to obtain employment and reintegrate into the community.

Source: Rachel King, "Sex Offender Registries: Public Safety or Public Hazard?" *Oldspeak*, May 18, 2006. Available online, http://www.rutherford.org/Oldspeak/Articles/Law/oldspeak-sexregistries.asp.

Registration and Notification Laws Are Unconstitutional

since notification may simply give some neighbors time to thwart the plans."[22]

Consider another, more recent case that had worse consequences: A 20-year-old man from Nova Scotia accessed the database showing certain sex offenders in Maine, and looked up the home addresses for 32 different sex offenders. The man visited four different homes where sex offenders lived, and murdered two of them. This case of vigilantism is not unique.[23]

Megan's Laws impose registration and notification requirements on convicted sex offenders. State laws now must allow people online access to information about sex offenders. The net result is that people who have served their prison terms are now branded with a Scarlet Letter for the rest of their lives. They do not have the freedom to live, work, and repair their lives.

Patty Wetterling, the mother of Jacob Wetterling, whose disappearance at the hands of a sex offender inspired the 1994 federal law, believes that sex offender laws often go too far: "Many states make former offenders register for life, restrict where they can live, and make their details known to the public. And yet the evidence suggests these laws may do more harm than good."[24] Megan's Laws initially were passed to inform parents when a convicted sex offender was moving near their home. Wetterling points out that "the law has been expanded so that now anyone with an Internet connection can download details about almost any offender, whether or not they pose a risk, and whether or not they live nearby."[25] Commentator Sarah Tofte adds, "Subjecting convicted sex offenders to community notification for the rest of their lives may do great harm—both to the individuals and to community safety. Offenders included on online sex offender registries endure shattered privacy, social ostracism, diminished employment opportunities, harassment, and even vigilante violence. Their families suffer as well."[26]

Many of the registration laws fail to take into account differences between sex offenders.

One of the biggest flaws with Internet registration and notification laws is that they simply fail to take into account the dramatic differences between different types of sex offenders. Take the example of a 50-year-old man who rapes a 10-year-old girl; that individual can fairly be characterized as a sexual predator. Then, however, consider the example of an 18-year-old man who has consensual sex with a 15-year-old girl and is convicted of statutory rape. He also is labeled as a sex offender. People may assume that this individual is also a pedophile when in reality he was a young man who used poor judgment in his relationships.

A man known only as Jameel M. explained his predicament to the Human Rights Watch for their insightful report "No Easy Answers: Sex Offender Laws in the United States." The man wrote:

> When people see my picture on the state sex offender registry they assume I am a pedophile. I have been called a baby rapist by my neighbors; feces have been left on my driveway; a stone with a note wrapped around it telling me to "watch my back" was thrown through my window, almost hitting a guest. What the registry doesn't tell people is that I was convicted at age 17 of sex with my 14-year-old girlfriend, that I have been offense-free for over a decade, that I have completed my therapy, and that the judge and my probation officer didn't even think I was at risk of reoffending. My life is in ruins, not because I had sex as a teenager, and not because I was convicted, but because of how my neighbors have reacted to the information on the Internet.[27]

The Human Rights Watch report explains that "in many states, people who urinate in public, teenagers who have consensual sex with each other, adults who sell sex to other adults, and

Registration and Notification Laws Are Unconstitutional

kids who expose themselves as a prank are required to register as sex offenders."[28] Howard University Law School professor Rachel King recommends that "states should differentiate between serious and non-serious offenders and only require registration of the most serious offenders."[29]

Megan's Laws are based on false assumptions about sex offenders.

Megan's Laws are based on the premise that sex offenders reoffend regularly—even after incarceration and release—and that sex offenses are often committed by strangers. These are more myths than realities. First, the recidivism rates of sex offenders are much lower than originally thought. A 2003 Bureau of Justice Statistics study showed that only 5 percent of sex offenders committed another sex crime within three years of their release from state prison. The study found that "sex offenders were less likely than non-sex offenders to be rearrested for any offense—43 percent of sex offenders versus 68 percent of non-sex offenders."[30] A 1997 U.S. Department of Justice study found that 87 percent of sex offenders had never been arrested for a previous sex offense. Also according to the study, 3 out of 4 violent sex offenders do not commit a sex crime again.[31]

The reality is that research on the recidivism of sex offenders is mixed. Author Anne-Marie McAlinden writes: "Indeed, despite this shared perception that recidivism is a more serious problem among sex offenders than other criminals, recidivism research over the last few decades has produced mixed results."[32] Sex offenders do not have as high a recidivism rate as drug dealers or burglars or many other types of criminals. "The perception of increased and inevitable dangerousness and re-offense is not true," writes author Michelle Meloy. "In the most simplistic of comparisons (sex offenders versus other serious criminals), recidivism rates are significantly lower among men who sexually offend than among other types of serious and violent criminals."[33] The media demonizes sex offenders with sensational news reports, which helps politicians drum up support for laws, but it does not address underlying issues. Rather than

Human Rights Watch Study on Recidivism of Sex Offenders

Some of the false impressions about the rates at which sex offenders recidivate may have originated with calculations by the Bureau of Justice Statistics (BJS) as to the relative likelihood at which released prisoners would be rearrested for the same type of crime as that for which they had been in prison. In a study published in 1997 based on prisoners released in 1983, the BJS calculated that relative to other offenders, a rapist was 10.5 times more likely than other released prisoners to be rearrested for another rape. More recently, based on a study of prisoners released in 1994, the BJS calculated a rapist's likelihood of being rearrested for another rape as 4.2 times a non-rapist's odds.

But the odds of 10.5 or 4.2 do *not* mean that rapists' rates of recidivism are 10.5 or 4.2 times greater than the recidivism rates of other offenders. The figures are properly understood as indicating the "degree of specializing" that is apparent among many offenders. For example, according to the BJS, a robber is 2.7 times more likely to be rearrested for another robbery as compared to an offender who had not been serving time for a robbery.

Furthermore, specialization is not absolute; non-rapists are also rearrested on rape charges. For example, 1.2 percent of the prisoners who had been serving time for robbery were rearrested for rape. Indeed, in the three-year post-release period, people who had been serving time for rape were responsible for only 4.8 percent of the rapes committed by all prisoners released in 1994.

Most prisoners who are going to break the law again do so fairly soon after their release from prison. This is also true for sex offenders. For example, according to the Bureau of Justice Statistics, during the three years following release from prison in 1994, 40 percent of the arrests for new sex crimes committed by released sex offenders occurred in the first year. In Ohio, of all sex offenders who went back to prison for a new sex offense within a 10-year post-release period, one-half did so within two years, and two-thirds within three years.

Registration and Notification Laws Are Unconstitutional

obsessively focus on condemning sex offenders, more attention should be centered on treatment and understanding of the root causes of sex offenses.

The other side of that is that the longer someone remains offense-free in the community, the less likely he or she will commit another offense. This is true for people who have committed sex offenses as well as other kinds of crimes. For example, the 2004 survey of sex offender recidivism studies cited above indicated that an average of 20 percent of all sex offenders would be arrested or convicted for another sex offense over a 10-year period after being released into the community. For offenders who remained offense-free for 5 years, their recidivism rate for the next 10 years declined to 12 percent. For those who remained offense-free for 10 years, their recidivism rate over the next 5 years declined even further, to 9 percent. After 15 years offense-free, the recidivism rate for the next 5 years was 4 percent.

A number of other factors are also linked to recidivism, including the relationship of the victim to the offender. Offenders whose victims were within their own family recidivate at a significantly lower rate than offenders whose victims were outside of their family. For all child molesters, the lowest recidivism rates were for those who abused family members—13 percent after 15 years living in the community. The age at which a sex offender commits the sex offense also has a substantial association with recidivism. Offenders older than 50 when released from prison had half the recidivism rate of those younger than 50: 12 percent versus 26 percent, respectively, after 15 years.

Some experts who specialize in the treatment of these individuals are not surprised that convicted sex offenders have a relatively low recidivism rate. As one treatment provider told Human Rights Watch, "When an individual is caught and held accountable for his behavior, he often becomes motivated to get better. His behavior is no longer a secret, and it becomes a reckoning point for him—he must decide whether he is going to change his behavior, or face the consequences."

Source: Human Rights Watch, "No Easy Answers: Sex Offenders in the United States," September 2007. Available online at http://www.hrw.org/reports/2007/us0907/4.htm#_Toc176672567.

Summary

Sex offender registration and notification laws are based on the false premise that they provide greater security. Nothing shows that this is true, and, in fact, these laws may cause greater harm than good. Numerous cases of vigilantism have led to violence against sex offenders who had served their time in prison and were released into the community.

Furthermore, the notification laws fail to properly delineate between different types of sex offenders. Although newer laws are creating new tiers of sex offenders, the problem remains that the definition of a sex offender is quite broad. An older teenager who has consensual sex with a younger teenager simply should not be lumped together with a violent sexual predator.

Notification laws place a permanent Scarlet Letter on the backs of sex offenders. They reduce them to public shaming and stigmatization, often for the rest of their lives. A majority of these sex offenders will not reoffend. Yet, they are branded for life.

Residency Restrictions Are a Constitutional Way to Protect Victims from Sex Offenders

Megan Kanka was murdered by a convicted sex offender who lived right across the street. Jessica Lunsford was murdered by a convicted sex offender who lived in a trailer right near her home. The awful reality is that many more children have been sexually abused or harmed by convicted sex offenders who live a stone's throw away from them. For this reason, having residency restrictions against sex offenders is not only a good idea—it is morally required.

Courts have upheld residency restrictions.
The 8th U.S. Circuit Court of Appeals upheld an Iowa law that prohibits certain convicted sex offenders from living within 2,000 feet (610 meters) of a school or registered childcare facility. The law did not apply to those sex offenders who lived there prior to the enactment of the law.

Three convicted sex offenders sued, contending that the law violated their constitutional rights, but the federal appeals court rejected their arguments. An expert witness testified in the litigation that "reducing the opportunity and the temptation to reoffend is extremely important to treatment."[34] The expert explained that it was a commonsense measure to deny convicted sex offenders access to places frequented by children. Another expert testified that there is a "legitimate public safety concern" in where convicted sex offenders reside.[35]

THE LETTER OF THE LAW

Iowa's Residency Restriction on Sex Offenders

692A.2A Residency restrictions—childcare facilities and schools.

1. For purposes of this section, *"person"* means a person who has committed a criminal offense against a minor, or an aggravated offense, sexually violent offense, or other relevant offense that involved a minor.
2. A person shall not reside within 2,000 feet of the real property comprising a public or nonpublic elementary or secondary school or a childcare facility.
3. A person who resides within 2,000 feet of the real property comprising a public or nonpublic elementary or secondary school, or a childcare facility, commits an aggravated misdemeanor.
4. A person residing within 2,000 feet of the real property comprising a public or nonpublic elementary or secondary school or a childcare facility does not commit a violation of this section if any of the following apply:
    a. The person is required to serve a sentence at a jail, prison, juvenile facility, or other correctional institution or facility.
    b. The person is subject to an order of commitment under chapter 229A.
    c. The person has established a residence prior to July 1, 2002, or a school or childcare facility is newly located on or after July 1, 2002.
    d. The person is a minor or a ward under a guardianship.

Source: Iowa Code § 692A.2A

Residency Restrictions Are Constitutional

The plaintiffs in the case attempted to argue that the residency restriction infringed on their due-process rights, their fundamental right to travel, and fundamental right to live where they want. The appeals court rejected those arguments, finding

FROM THE BENCH

Doe v. Miller (8th Cir. 2005)

The Does contend, however, that the statute is irrational because there is no scientific study that supports the legislature's conclusion that excluding sex offenders from residing within 2,000 feet of a school or childcare facility is likely to enhance the safety of children.

We reject this contention because we think it understates the authority of a state legislature to make judgments about the best means to protect the health and welfare of its citizens in an area where precise statistical data is unavailable and human behavior is necessarily unpredictable.... There can be no doubt of a legislature's rationality in believing that sex offenders are a serious threat in this Nation and that when convicted sex offenders reenter society, they are much more likely than any other type of offender to be re-arrested for a new rape or sexual assault....

The legislature is institutionally equipped to weigh the benefits and burdens of various distances, and to reconsider its initial decision in light of experience and data accumulated over time....

Sex offenders have a high rate of recidivism, and the parties presented expert testimony that reducing opportunity and temptation is important to minimizing the risk of reoffense. Even experts in the field could not predict with confidence whether a particular sex offender will reoffend, whether an offender convicted of an offense against a teenager will be among those who "cross over" to offend against a younger child, or the degree to which regular proximity to a place where children are located enhances the risk of reoffense against children. One expert in the district court opined that it is just "common sense" that limiting the frequency of contact between sex offenders and areas where children are located is likely to reduce the risk of an offense. The policymakers of Iowa are entitled to employ such "common sense," and we are not persuaded that the means selected to pursue the State's legitimate interest are without rational basis.

Source: *Doe v. Miller*, 405 F.3d 700, 714–716 (8th Cir. 2005).

that the statute did not implicate any fundamental right. In constitutional law, restrictions on fundamental rights are subject to the highest form of judicial review, while restrictions that don't involve fundamental rights are subject to a lower form of judicial review called rational basis. This means that the legislature must simply have had a rational, nonarbitrary reason for passing the law.

The 8th U.S. Circuit Court of Appeals determined that the Iowa residency restriction did not involve any fundamental rights of the convicted sex offenders. Thus, they evaluated the law under a rational basis standard of review.

The plaintiffs also argued that the residency requirement was comparable to an extreme form of punishment long since

THE LETTER OF THE LAW

Residency Restriction in Arkansas

5–14–128. Registered offender living near school, public park, youth center, or daycare prohibited.
(a) It is unlawful for a sex offender who is required to register under the Sex Offender Registration Act of 1997, § 12–12–901 et seq., and who has been assessed as a Level 3 or Level 4 offender to reside within two thousand feet (2,000′) of the property on which any public or private elementary or secondary school, public park, youth center, or daycare facility is located.
(b) (1) It is not a violation of this section if the property on which the sex offender resides is owned and occupied by the sex offender and was purchased prior to the date on which the public or private elementary or secondary school, public park, youth center, or daycare facility was established.
(2) The exclusion in subdivision (b)(1) of this section does not apply to a sex offender who pleads guilty or nolo contendere to or is found guilty of another sex offense after the public or private elementary or secondary school, public park, youth center, or daycare facility is established.
(c) (1) (A) With respect to a public or private elementary or secondary school or a daycare facility, it is not a violation of this section if the sex offender resides on property he or she owns prior to July 16, 2003.

Residency Restrictions Are Constitutional

rejected in U.S. jurisprudence: banishment. The appeals court rejected the comparison, noting that the Iowa law did not have nearly the same punitive effect as banishment. "With respect to many offenders, the statute does not even require a change in residence," the court wrote, noting the grandfather provision that provided protection for those offenders who lived in their residences within the requisite distance of schools or childcare facilities before July 1, 2002.[36] The appeals court added that "the evidence presented at trial suggested that convicted sex offenders as a class were more likely to commit sex offenses against minors than the general population."[37]

Other courts have upheld residency restrictions. In *Weems v. Little Rock Police Department* (2006), the 8th U.S. Circuit Court

---

(B) With respect to a public park or youth center, it is not a violation of this section if the sex offender resides on property he or she owns prior to July 31, 2007.
(2) (A) The exclusion in subdivision (c)(1)(A) of this section does not apply to a sex offender who pleads guilty or nolo contendere to or is found guilty of another sex offense after July 16, 2003.
(B) The exclusion in subdivision (c)(1)(B) of this section does not apply to a sex offender who pleads guilty or nolo contendere to or is found guilty of another sex offense on or after July 31, 2007.
(d) A sex offender who is required to register under the Sex Offender Registration Act of 1997, § 12–12–901 et seq., and who knowingly violates a provision of this section is guilty of a Class D felony.
(e) As used in this section:
(1) "Public park" means any property owned or maintained by this state or a county, city, or town in this state for the recreational use of the public; and
(2) "Youth center" means any building, structure, or facility owned or operated by a not-for-profit organization or by this state or a county, city, or town in this state for use by minors to promote the health, safety, or general welfare of the minors.

Source: Arkansas Code Annotated § 5–14–128

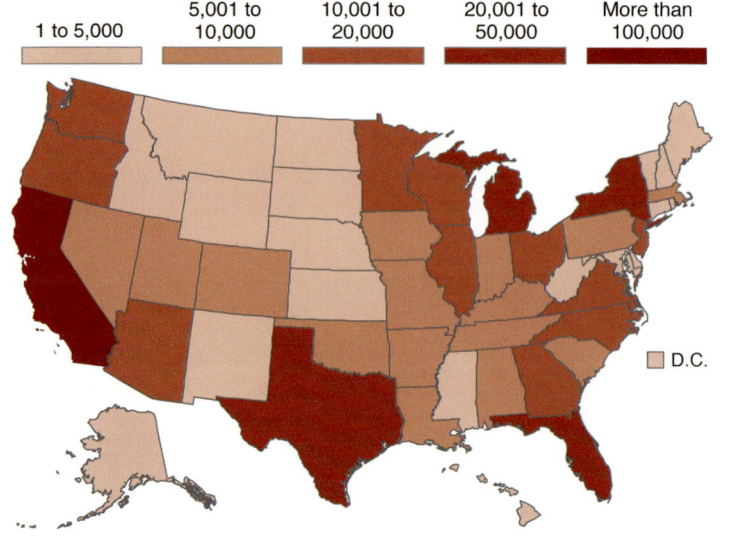

600,000 sex offenders across U.S.

California has the largest population of registered sex offenders in the U.S. – totaling nearly 20 percent of all registrants.

SOURCE: National Center for Missing & Exploited Children AP

There are over 600,000 registered sex offenders across the United States. This graphic shows their distribution by state.

of Appeals upheld an Arkansas law that also provided that certain sex offenders could not live within 2,000 feet of a school or youth center.[38]

The Arkansas law did not apply to all sex offenders—only to those adjudged to be Level 3 or Level 4 offenders. The Arkansas law did, however, apply to more than sex offenders who had harmed children (unlike the Iowa law upheld in *Doe v. Miller*). Two convicted sex offenders contended that the Arkansas law violated the equal protection clause because it treated certain convicted sex offenders worse than other sex offenders. The basic

FROM THE BENCH

Federal Court Explains Why the Risk Assessment Process for Sex Offenders is Constitutional

The State has a strong interest in protecting children from dangerous offenders through a process that is efficient and practical. While sex offenders have an interest in avoiding inaccurate community notification or an unwarranted residency restriction, the Guidelines do not permit notification of a "high risk" assessment, which triggers the residency restriction and may bring greater opprobrium than notification in accordance with Level 1 or 2 status, until after the conclusion of an administrative review. Prior to this review, the risk of erroneous deprivation is negligible. Although examiners believe that the offender is a "high risk," the community may be notified only that the offender presents a "moderate risk," and the offender's criminal record—which almost certainly implies at least some level of risk—is already a matter of public record. The administrative review then ensures that the sex offender's assessment is considered by both the examination team and the Sex Offender Review Committee before a Level 3 assessment is implemented....

Weems and Briggs complain primarily that the procedures do not afford the "rigors of an adversarial process," including a right to counsel and to confront witnesses against them, and that the risk assessment process includes "undefined and non-specific overrides and departures." We are not persuaded that these features make the process constitutionally inadequate. The Committee's assessment is designed to be thorough and complex, drawing on historical records, psychological evaluations, and actuarial techniques. Deviations from the actuarial prediction models are designed to be "used sparingly," only with the approval of "senior clinical staff," and are subject to review by the Sex Offender Assessment Committee. (*Guidelines*, at 14–15.) These "overrides" and "departures" are not necessarily unfavorable to an offender; they may either increase or decrease the risk level assigned. Given the difficulty of predicting human behavior and the numerous variables that may influence a professional's predictive judgment in a particular case, we do not think the authority to vary from the actuarial models or the absence of a precise listing of circumstances that will justify a variance are unconstitutionally vague or otherwise inconsistent with the tenets of procedural due process. Indeed, it is just as likely that the flexibility to consider individual circumstances in special cases, rather than to follow a rigid actuarial model in every case, actually *reduces* the risk of an erroneous deprivation.

Source: *Weems v. Little Rock Police Department*, 453 F.3d 1010, (8th Cir. 2006) 1018-1019.

premise of the equal protection clause is that similarly situated individuals should be treated equally. Equal protection concerns come into play when one group is treated much worse than another class of persons. The 8th Circuit rejected that argument, saying it was rational for the Arkansas legislature to make distinctions between sex offenders based on their dangerousness.[39]

The offenders also argued that the risk assessment process that assigned offenders to particular levels of dangerousness was flawed, and that it violated their due-process rights. The federal court rejected that argument as well, noting that a team of evaluators "conducts a thorough review of official records and historical data, performs psychological testing and evaluation, undertakes actuarial analyses, and conducts a personal interview with the offender."[40]

In *People v. Leroy*, an Illinois appeals court rejected the challenges of a convicted child sex offender who lived with his mother within 500 feet (152 meters) of an elementary school. Illinois had a sex offender registry law that prohibited sex offenders from residing within 500 feet of a playground or other facility that provides exclusive services to children.[41] Leroy, 36 years old, had lived in the house with his mother all his life and contended that the application of the law to him therefore violated his due-process rights. The state appeals court rejected this claim, writing that the law "bears a reasonable relationship to the goal of protecting children from known child sex offenders and sets forth a reasonable method of furthering that goal."[42]

There is a clear precedent allowing residency restrictions.

In 1995, Florida became the first state to pass a residency restriction on convicted child sex offenders. Now, nearly 30 states have such laws. They range in distance requirements from 500 feet (152 meters) in South Dakota to 2,000 feet (610 meters) in several other states such as Alabama and Oklahoma. Numerous cities across the country have also enacted residential restrictions on convicted sex offenders.

It is true that there is a shortage of social science literature to prove that residency restrictions will make children safer. This is partly because the laws are so new. It is impossible to prove anything definitively when the laws haven't been in existence very long. (Additionally, just because a law is in existence does not mean that it is being properly enforced.)

Still, social science literature is not necessary to prove that residency restrictions on sex offenders will have a positive impact. Common sense is enough. These are important, common sense measures. Instead of wasting time worrying whether convicted sex offenders will have enough places to live, more attention should be paid to protecting children. Editorial writer David Yepsen wrote persuasively when discussing the political opposition to Iowa's residency restriction of 2,000 feet: "Where are these people going to live? Soon there won't be any place for them in Iowa. Exactly. Get them out of here. Their crimes are so heinous and so twisted that Iowans are deciding these people are unfit to live among the rest of us. Since the experts can't agree on whether treatment for sex offenders does any good, decent people are simply unwilling to take chances."[43]

If a child sex offender lives close to children, he or she can more easily molest them. Jesse Timmendequas lived right across the street from Megan Kanka. John Couey lived nearly next door to Jessica Lunsford. It can't be proven, but there is a good chance that if there had been a residency restriction in place and enforced in those locales, Megan and Jessica might still be alive.

COUNTERPOINT

Residency Restrictions Against Sexual Offenders Violate Constitutional Rights

> Neither states nor localities should have residency restriction laws that apply to entire classes of former offenders. Authorized residency restrictions should be limited to individually tailored restrictions for certain offenders as a condition of the terms of his or her probation, parole, or other mandated supervision.
>
> —Human Rights Watch (2007 study)[44]

A woman in her thirties made a mistake 20 years ago that appeared harmless to her at the time. As a teen, she had oral sex with her 14-year-old boyfriend. Even though the sexual act was consensual, the girl, as the older minor, was charged and convicted of statutory rape. For the rest of her life, she bore the Scarlet Letter of being a sex offender. She had to register her

Residency Restrictions Violate Constitutional Rights

whereabouts with authorities and her picture was plastered up on an Internet registry site for the world to access. She also may not be able to live in her childhood home because of residency restrictions.

Even though this adult woman poses no real threat to any children—in fact, she has two children of her own—she is considered a sex offender who may be subject to a law that severely limits where she can legally live. This may sound like a wild, imaginative, hypothetical situation, but it is not. It is a nightmarish reality for some convicted sex offenders.

Janet Allison, a mother of five in Georgia, was arrested because she had allowed her pregnant 15-year-old daughter's 17-year-old boyfriend to move in with the family. This earned Allison a conviction for being a party to child molestation. Because of a sex offender registration requirement, she was also forced to move from her home in Dahlonega, Georgia, because her two-bedroom mobile home was too close to a church.[45]

Many states and towns have passed heavy restrictions on where sex offenders can live and work. In effect, those towns have created what legal commentator Julie Hilden has called "pedophile-free zones."[46] At least 27 states and hundreds of cities have passed such politically popular laws.[47] The strictest of these restrictions prohibit individuals from living in homes that they have lived in for years: Some of these laws don't even have an exception for an offender who lives in his home legally and then must move because a day-care center, skating rink, church, or school opens within a certain distance.

Some of these laws were passed for the purpose of protecting minors, but they do more harm than good. In a recent study, Human Rights Watch reported: "In many cases, residency restrictions have the effect of banishing registrants from entire urban areas and forcing them to live far from their homes and families."[48]

Residency restrictions do not make children any safer.

Ironically, the residency restrictions on sex offenders do not make children any safer. Studies indicate that, if anything, these restrictions may place children in even greater danger. "There is no evidence that residency restrictions work, and there are some pretty good arguments why they are not likely to be effective," says David Finkelhor, director of the Crimes Against Children Research Center at the University of New Hampshire. "No one who has any real professional experience in the management of sex offenders thinks these laws make much sense."[49]

One of the problems is that many sex offenses are committed against children by relatives or acquaintances of the children—not by a stranger. The residency restriction laws are obsessed with the phenomenon of "stranger danger" when the reality is that most of the harm is perpetrated by older family members. Many of these crimes go unreported. Furthering the argument against residency restrictions is the fact that the recidivism rate for most people labeled as sex offenders is actually much lower than what many people believe—lower than that for drug offenders or thieves.

After examining hundreds of sex offenders and their case histories upon release, the Minnesota Department of Corrections concluded in an April 2007 study that residency restrictions would likely not deter future crimes. In its conclusion, the department wrote: "In general, the results here provide very little support for the notion that residency restriction laws would lower the incidence of sexual recidivism, particularly among child molesters."[50] The report explains that most child molesters intentionally seek a victim who lives at least a mile away so that there is less of a chance of being recognized. This defeats the purpose of most residency restriction laws.

Even prosecutors and state police organizations have called for the relaxation or abolition of residency restriction laws. The

Residency Restrictions Violate Constitutional Rights

Picketers stand in front of a house where a convicted sex offender was supposed to live. Critics of online offender registries say that public access to such information means that offenders may be subject to harassment even after they have served their sentences.

Iowa County Attorneys Association (a group of district attorneys responsible for enforcing the laws) released a statement in 2006 explaining why they opposed the state's restrictive law that prevents sex offenders from living within 2,000 feet (610 meters) of various places frequented by children. The statement read in part: "Research indicates that there is no correlation between residency restrictions and reducing sex offenses against children or improving the safety of children."[51]

The attorneys also explained that the broad residency restriction law actually might harm children because it prompts many sex offenders to attempt to avoid law enforcement. The association explains:

> Law enforcement has observed that the residency restriction is causing offenders to become homeless, to change residences without notifying authorities of their new location, to register false addresses or to simply disappear. If they do not register, law enforcement and the public do not know where they are living. The resulting damage to the reliability of the sex offender registry does not serve the interests of public safety.[52]

Residency restrictions are unconstitutional.

Residency restriction laws represent bad policy with several unintended, damaging consequences. Many of the laws also violate offenders' constitutional rights. For example, the Georgia Supreme Court recently ruled that the state's law that prohibited registered sex offenders from living within 1,000 feet (305 meters) of various locations violated the Fifth Amendment by "taking" the offender's property without "just compensation."

The problem is that Georgia's law did not provide for the situation when a sex offender is lawfully residing in his residence and then a day care or elementary school or church locates within close proximity of the offender's home. Even though the offender was living there first, the terms of the residency restriction now force the offender to move because a day care has opened up within 1,000 feet of his home. This is what happened to registered sex offender Anthony Mann in Georgia. He lived in his home according to the law and then a day care center opened near his home. The Georgia Supreme Court invalidated its residency restriction law in *Mann v. Department of Corrections*.[53] The court explained that the law's lack of a "move-to-the-offender" exception created a problem: "Sex offenders face the possibility of being repeatedly uprooted and forced to abandon homes in order to comply with the restrictions" in the Georgia law.[54]

The Georgia court noted that third parties could determine the home address of a sex offender and then deliberately try to open up a daycare, school, or church within close proximity of the offender "for the specific purpose of using [the Georgia law] to force the offender out of the community."[55]

The residency restrictions are also impermissible ex post facto laws. Article I, Section 10 of the U.S. Constitution prohibits ex post facto laws, which increase punishment for a crime after the fact, when the original conduct did not constitute a crime or called for a different punishment. The residency restrictions on sex offenders are ex post facto laws because they impose far harsher penalties on sex offenders long after they have already served the time for their crime. Circuit Judge Michael Melloy articulated this view in his dissenting opinion in *Doe v. Miller*

FROM THE BENCH

Mann v. Department of Corrections (2007)

Moreover, OCGA § 42–1-15 looms over every location appellant [the sex offender in question] chooses to call home, with its ongoing potential to force appellant from each new residence whenever, within that statutory 1,000-foot buffer zone, some third party chooses to establish any of the long list of places and facilities encompassed within the residency restriction. While this time it was a daycare center, next time it could be a playground, a school bus stop, a skating rink, or a church. OCGA § 41–1-15 does not merely interfere with, it positively precludes appellant from having any reasonable investment-backed expectation in any property purchased as his private residence....

Moreover, we must recognize that OCGA § 42–1-15 effectively places the State's police power into the hands of private third parties, enabling them to force a registered sex offender like appellant, under penalty of a minimum 10-year sentence for commission of a felony, to forfeit valuable property rights in his legally purchased home.

Source: *Mann v. Department of Corrections*, decision available online at http://www.gasupreme.us/pdf/s07a1043.pdf.

(2005), when the majority of the 8th U.S. Circuit Court of Appeals upheld Iowa's 2,000-foot (610-meter) residency requirement.[56] Judge Melloy compared the law to banishment. He wrote: "There are so few legal housing options that many offenders face the choice of living in rural areas or leaving the state. The difficulty in finding proper housing effectively prevents offenders from living in many Iowa communities. This effectively results in banishment from virtually all of Iowa's cities and larger towns."[57]

An Indiana appeals court invalidated a sex offender residency law that would have required a convicted sex offender to move from his home that he had lived in for more than 20 years with his wife.[58] The state contended that he violated the law by remaining within 1,000 feet (305 meters) of a school. The appeals court found that the law "impinges upon one of this country's most closely held rights, the right to property."[59] The court explained that the residency restriction was not in place at the time of this man's conviction, and "to apply that statute now would affect his substantial rights in his property since it would prevent him from residing in his home and using his property."[60]

The laws also present fundamental problems for due process. The Fifth and Fourteenth Amendments prohibit government officials from infringing on individuals' "life, liberty, or property interests without due process of law." This prevents the government from passing laws that are unreasonable and arbitrary, or laws that "shock the conscience." It is at least arguable that some of the stricter residency restriction laws would fall into that category.

Summary

Residency restrictions on sex offenders are politically popular legislative moves that do not advance the purported goal of protecting minors. Simply put, these restrictions are bad policy and bad law. Most sex offenders are not complete strangers to their victims; they are family members or close friends who gain willing access to the victim's life. The phenomenon of "stranger

Residency Restrictions Violate Constitutional Rights

danger," while creating sensationalism for the media, does not accurately depict reality.

Furthermore, the restrictive laws will not lead to increased safety because the laws make it more likely that a sex offender will not register, or will move out to rural areas where he or she cannot be monitored or treated as effectively. Stated simply, more sex offenders would register if they did not have such strict laws against where they could live. It follows that if more sex offenders register, society will have an easier time monitoring these people and, perhaps, ensuring they receive treatment. Legal commentator Meghan Sil Towers explains: "Residence restrictions, while facially attractive, are unduly burdensome to both registered sex offenders and the communities that must eventually receive them. The presence of other methods of managing convicted sex offenders makes residence restrictions look even less attractive."[61]

Residency requirement laws also violate the constitutional rights of the offenders. Many of the laws constitute an unlawful "taking" of property within the meaning of the Fifth Amendment. The laws also increase punishment after the fact, qualifying them as unconstitutional ex post facto laws.

At the very least, the residency restrictions should be modified to apply to only a very narrow class of sexually violent offenders who have shown a capacity to reoffend. More evidence needs to be established showing that even those measures would actually have a positive effect. Human Rights Watch concludes: "We are also convinced that there is no legitimate basis for blanket residency restrictions. We do not object to time-limited restrictions that are imposed on individual offenders on a case-by-case basis, for example, as a condition of parole. But a wholesale banishment of a class of individuals should have no place in the United States."[62]

Civil Commitment of Violent Sexual Predators Is Necessary and Constitutional

Some sexual predators attack again when given the opportunity. They seemingly cannot or will not help themselves, and so continue to prey on innocent children. They are imminent dangers to the community who must be stopped.

Consider the 1989 case of Earl Shriner, a mentally challenged man who, two years after his release from prison, sexually abused and mutilated a seven-year-old boy and left him for dead. Shriner had a long history of sex crimes and attacks against children, and made his feelings about his crimes known in prison before his release. Unfortunately, the state had no way to keep Shriner incarcerated once he had served his criminal sentence.[63] Shriner's awful crime spurred the Washington state legislature into action. The very next year, the state passed a law that authorized the civil containment of certain sexually violent predators. The law became the model for similar legislation in other states.

Another such sexual predator case reached the U.S. Supreme Court. It involved a man in Kansas named Leroy Hendricks who had a long history of committing sexual offenses involving young children.

In 1955, Leroy Hendricks exposed his genitals to two young girls, later pleading guilty to indecent exposure. Two years later, in 1957, he pleaded guilty to the crime of lewdness and received a short jail sentence. In 1960, he molested two young boys at a

Legal Language: Findings of the Washington Legislature for its Sexually Violent Predator Law

§ 71.09.010. Findings

The legislature finds that a small but extremely dangerous group of sexually violent predators exist who do not have a mental disease or defect that renders them appropriate for the existing involuntary treatment act, chapter 71.05 RCW, which is intended to be a short-term civil commitment system that is primarily designed to provide short-term treatment to individuals with serious mental disorders and then return them to the community. In contrast to persons appropriate for civil commitment under chapter 71.05 RCW, sexually violent predators generally have personality disorders and/or mental abnormalities which are unamenable to existing mental illness treatment modalities and those conditions render them likely to engage in sexually violent behavior. The legislature further finds that sex offenders' likelihood of engaging in repeat acts of predatory sexual violence is high. The existing involuntary commitment act, chapter 71.05 RCW, is inadequate to address the risk to reoffend because during confinement these offenders do not have access to potential victims and therefore they will not engage in an overt act during confinement as required by the involuntary treatment act for continued confinement. The legislature further finds that the prognosis for curing sexually violent offenders is poor, the treatment needs of this population are very long term, and the treatment modalities for this population are very different than the traditional treatment modalities for people appropriate for commitment under the involuntary treatment act.

Source: Rev. Code Wash. (ARCW) § 71.09.010 (2008).

carnival. He later molested a 7-year-old girl. He then sexually assaulted another young boy and fondled an 11-year-old girl. He was imprisoned again in 1967 but refused treatment as a sex offender. Diagnosed as a pedophile, Hendricks received some treatment, which he discontinued after his release in 1972. He later sexually abused his own stepdaughter and stepson. Later still, he was convicted of "taking indecent liberties" with two 13-year-old boys.[64]

Hendricks was convicted of these latest offenses in 1984 and served time in prison. In 1994, Hendricks finished serving his time and came up for conditional release. He was slated for release to a halfway house. The state of Kansas, however, recognized Hendricks's repeated acts of sexual offenses against children. The state thus began civil commitment proceedings against him in agreement with the state Sexually Violent Predator Act of 1994, which was modeled on the Washington law.[65] The preamble to the Kansas law provides: "The legislature further finds that sexually violent predators' likelihood of engaging in repeat acts of predatory sexual violence is high. The existing involuntary commitment procedure is inadequate to address the risk these sexually violent predators pose to society."

The state filed a petition that led to the continued confinement of Leroy Hendricks even after he had served his prison term. This may seem unfair to some civil libertarians because Hendricks had served his time and was scheduled for release, but society has a duty to protect young children from sexually violent predators. The greater good of protecting children outweighs the personal rights of sex offenders.

The U.S. Supreme Court agreed with this argument and in its 1997 decision in *Kansas v. Hendricks*, it upheld the constitutionality of the Kansas Sexually Violent Predator Act of 1994.

Involuntary civil commitment proceedings have a long history.

Civil commitment laws were common during the eighteenth and nineteenth centuries. For example, a 1788 law in New York permitted the confinement of those individuals who were "furiously mad." In his opinion in the *Hendricks* case, Justice Clarence Thomas wrote: "We have consistently upheld such involuntary commitment statutes provided the confinement takes place pursuant to proper procedures and evidentiary standards."[66]

Legal experts recognize the need for the civil commitment of certain individuals with mental illnesses. In 1905, the U.S. Supreme Court explained: "There are manifold restraints to which every person is necessarily subject for the common good. On any other basis organized society could not exist with safety to its members."[67] Even after they have served a criminal sentence, some individuals are simply not equipped to enter regular society. Their mental and personal issues will likely cause them to harm themselves or others. The process of civil commitment is a recognized process that is also applied to sexually violent predators.

The U.S. Supreme Court upheld a 1939 Minnesota law that permitted a juvenile court's civil commitment of a man with "psychopathic personality." The court explained in *Minnesota ex. rel. Pearson v. Probate Court of Ramsey Co.* (1940)[68] that Edwin Pearson displayed a continued course of misconduct in sexual matters and was, thus, subject to civil commitment.

In *Addington v. Texas* (1979), the U.S. Supreme Court ruled that mentally ill individuals who posed a danger to society could be civilly committed indefinitely as long as the commitment process met certain evidentiary standards. This meant that the state had to show by clear and convincing evidence that the individual was mentally ill and posed a danger to others. The *Addington* case involved a mentally ill young man who physically threatened his mother. The court, in an opinion by Chief Justice Warren E. Burger, explicitly stated that the state under its police powers has a strong interest in protecting society from dangerously mentally ill individuals.[69] The court also determined that the state did not have to meet the criminal law standard of "beyond a reasonable doubt" before instituting such civil commitment proceedings.

In *Heller v. Doe* (1993), the U.S. Supreme Court upheld a Kentucky law that allowed the civil commitment of mentally disabled persons who posed a danger to themselves or others.[70] Under this law, family members could file a petition seeking such commitment procedures for their relatives. If people with

FROM THE BENCH

Minnesota ex rel. Pearson v. Probate Court of Ramsey Co. (1940):

This construction of the statute destroys the contention that it is too vague and indefinite to constitute valid legislation. There must be proof of a "habitual course of misconduct in sexual matters" on the part of the persons against whom a proceeding under the statute is directed, which has shown "an utter lack of power to control their sexual impulses," and hence that they "are likely to attack or otherwise inflict injury, loss, pain, or other evil on the objects of their uncontrolled and uncontrollable desire." These underlying conditions, calling for evidence of past conduct pointing to probable consequences, are as susceptible of proof as many of the criteria constantly applied in prosecutions for crime....

Equally unavailing is the contention that the statute denies appellant the equal protection of the laws. The argument proceeds on the view that the statute has selected a group which is a part of a larger class. The question, however, is whether the legislature could constitutionally make a class of the group it did select. That is, whether there is any rational basis for such a selection. We see no reason for doubt upon this point. Whether the legislature could have gone further is not the question. The class it did select is identified by the state court in terms which clearly show that the persons within that class constitute a dangerous element in the community which the legislature in its discretion could put under appropriate control. As we have often said, the legislature is free to recognize degrees of harm, and it may confine its restrictions to those classes of cases where the need is deemed to be clearest. If the law "presumably hits the evil where it is most felt, it is not to be overthrown because there are other instances to which it might have been applied.

Source: *Minnesota ex. rel. Pearson v. Probate Court of Ramsey Co.*, 309 U.S. 270, 274–275 (1940).

dangerous mental problems can be put in civil confinement, so can the sexually violent predator who is clearly dangerous and may be able to wreak more harm on others.

Civil commitment proceedings against convicted sex offenders do not violate the Constitution.

The initiation of civil commitment proceedings for sexually violent offenders—even after such offenders have served their criminal sentences—does not violate constitutional principles. Sex offender Leroy Hendricks contended that the application of Kansas's sexually violent predator law violated the double jeopardy and ex post facto clauses of the Constitution. The double jeopardy clause is found in the Fifth Amendment and prohibits the state from instituting criminal prosecutions against an individual after that individual has been acquitted in a previous criminal trial.

In *Hendricks*, the court rejected the double jeopardy and ex post facto arguments advanced by the counsel for Hendricks because the civil commitment statute was a civil law, not a criminal one. Double jeopardy and ex post facto challenges are advanced against criminal laws with a punitive purpose. Justice Clarence Thomas, writing for the majority, determined that the

Legal Language: Double Jeopardy and Ex Post Facto

Double jeopardy clause: "Nor shall any person be subject for the same offense to be twice put in jeopardy of life or limb."

Ex post facto clause: "No bill of attainder or ex post facto law shall be passed."

Sources: Fifth Amendment to the U.S. Constitution and Article I, Section 9 of the U.S. Constitution

Kansas civil commitment law was not punitive. He noted that the two main justifications of criminal laws were retribution and deterrence.

Retribution did not apply to the Kansas civil commitment law because the law "does not affix culpability for prior criminal conduct."[71] Furthermore, the law does not require a prior criminal conviction before civil commitment. In other words, a person can be civilly committed even if she or he has not been convicted of a criminal offense and sentenced to prison. "An absence of the necessary criminal responsibility suggests that the State is not seeking retribution for a past misdeed," Thomas wrote.[72] Another reason the court rejected the double jeopardy claim was that criminal laws normally require knowing criminal intent (called *scienter*) on the part of the charged individual (the alleged criminal). The civil commitment law contains no such scienter requirement, meaning that a person can be committed under such a law based on a "mental abnormality" or "personality disorder" rather than any form of criminal intent.[73]

The Kansas law did not further the criminal law purpose of deterrence because individuals like Hendricks have disorders that prevent them from stopping their behavior. A natural justification for a criminal law is to deter or prevent people from ever reoffending. Some sex offenders have some sort of disorder that apparently prevents them from conforming their behavior within the confines of decent society. Thus, the rationale of deterrence does not apply to this law.[74]

Hendricks argued that double jeopardy applied even if the state of Kansas could show that the civil commitment law did not further the standard criminal-law justifications of retribution and deterrence. His argument was that the net effect of the law was still punitive. Justice Thomas dismissed that claim, noting that detention under civil commitment was not indefinite, but "only potentially indefinite."[75] Thomas offered other reasons for his opinion, including the fact that, if an individual showed he no longer suffered from the underlying disorder, he could be immediately released. Even then, according to Justice Thomas, "if an individual otherwise meets the requirements for involuntary civil commitment, the State is under no obligation to release that individual simply because the detention would follow a period of incarceration."[76]

In later decisions the Supreme Court has reaffirmed the basic guiding principle of the *Hendricks* decision. In *Seling v. Young* (2001), the court rejected the constitutional challenges filed by a sexually violent predator in Washington.[77] In *Kansas v. Crane* (2002), the Supreme Court ruled that state officials do not have to prove that an alleged sexually violent predator has a complete lack of control over his behavior before instituting civil commitment procedures.[78] "Insistence upon absolute lack of control would risk barring the civil commitment of highly dangerous persons suffering severe mental abnormalities," Justice Stephen Breyer wrote for the court.[79]

FROM THE BENCH

Justice Clarence Thomas on Why Civil Commitment Is Not Punitive

Where the State has "disavowed any punitive intent"; limited confinement to a small segment of particularly dangerous individuals; provided strict procedural safeguards; directed that confined persons be segregated from the general prison population and afforded the same status as others who have been civilly committed; recommended treatment if such is possible; and permitted immediate release upon a showing that the individual is no longer dangerous or mentally impaired, we cannot say that it acted with punitive intent. We therefore hold that the Act does not establish criminal proceedings and that involuntary confinement pursuant to the Act is not punitive. Our conclusion that the Act is nonpunitive thus removes an essential prerequisite for both Hendricks's double jeopardy and ex post facto claims.

Source: *Kansas v. Hendricks*, 521 U.S. 346, 368 (1997).

Summary

Sexually violent predators are dangerous individuals. Many of these individuals showcase a high degree of recidivism, meaning that they are likely to reoffend. The civil commitment of such individuals is not based on theory. It is based on the awful reality that some sex offenders continue to harm others. The United States has a long history of civil confinement of the dangerously mentally ill; every state has some form of such a statute. It is right to confine sexually violent offenders under these statutes.

The U.S. Supreme Court has ruled that it is indeed constitutional to civilly confine sexually violent predators after they complete their prison sentences. The court has ruled that these laws are not punitive, and therefore do not violate the Constitution's prohibitions against double jeopardy and ex post facto laws. The laws do not arbitrarily keep individuals locked up for minor offenses, and all state laws have procedures in place that afford individuals the opportunity to argue that they are not sexually violent predators.

Not all sex offenders should be confined civilly after their criminal offenses, but some should. This is a necessary provision to protect society. One legal commentator concludes: "Given the nature of sex crimes and the long term effects they cause their victims, we cannot release offenders who we know remain dangerous into society where they may strike again."[80]

COUNTERPOINT

Civil Commitment Proceedings Are Punitive and Violate Constitutional Rights

> American society has decided that there is no greater villain than the sex offender. Terrorists, drug dealers, murderers, kidnappers, mobsters, gangsters, drunk drivers, and white collar criminals do not elicit the emotions and evoke the political response that sex offenders do.[81]
> —Richard G. Wright, writing in the *New England Journal on Criminal and Civil Confinement*

A privately run center in Florida had the responsibility for housing and treating sex offenders who were committed to its institution after they had already served their sentences for their crimes. These individuals were deemed to be sexual predators under state law. The expectations were that they would receive some form of treatment; otherwise, these facilities would be nothing more than a second prison for the offenders.

Unfortunately, the treatment center failed miserably to provide much-needed help. The place turned into a cesspool of employee turnover, lack of security, drugs, and depression. The majority of the offenders did not even attend group therapy sessions. One inmate even escaped after a friend landed a helicopter inside the facility's yard. At one point an official with the company testified before the state legislature that she didn't know whether the place was supposed to be run like a treatment facility or a prison: "What is this place? Is it a prison? Is it a mental health center? A residential treatment facility where people are clients? What is it? We ask that question sometimes too. We really don't have a lot of guidance around what it is the state wants the facility to be, and we would encourage the state to look at that."[82] During its tenure, about 500 sex offenders were housed at the institution. Only one offender was recommended for release during that time frame. It was all such a failure that the privately owned center lost its state contract and was replaced.

Postincarceration "civil" confinement is in fact punitive.

Society's zeal to "commit" sex offenders after their prison terms is a politically popular measure that appeals to natural instincts. It is important not to pretend that committing someone after his sentence is anything other than punitive. Four justices on the U.S. Supreme Court in *Kansas v. Hendricks* understood this reality: that these measures are punitive, particularly when the individuals in question receive little or no treatment at all.[83] Hendricks is now more than 70 years old, confined to a wheelchair, and can barely move with a cane. He suffers from diabetes, has poor circulation, and has had a stroke. He finished his prison term nearly 15 years ago but remains confined, and will likely remain so for the rest of his life.[84]

Writing in dissent in the *Hendricks* case, Justice Stephen Breyer explained that the Kansas civil confinement law bore many striking resemblances to criminal punishment. He noted that many

FROM THE BENCH

Justice Stephen Breyer On Why the Kansas Civil Confinement Law Is Punitive

Conversely, a statutory scheme that provides confinement that does not reasonably fit a practically available, medically oriented treatment objective, more likely reflects a primarily punitive legislative purpose.... First, the State Supreme Court here ... has held that treatment is not a significant objective of the Act....

Second, the Kansas statute, insofar as it applies to previously convicted offenders such as Hendricks, commits, confines, and treats those offenders *after* they have served virtually their entire criminal sentence. That time-related circumstance seems deliberate. The Act explicitly defers diagnosis, evaluation, and commitment proceedings until a few weeks prior to the "anticipated release" of a previously convicted offender from prison. But why, one might ask, does the Act not commit and require treatment of sex offenders sooner, say, soon after they begin to serve their sentences....

Third, the statute, at least as of the time Kansas applied it to Hendricks, did not require the committing authority to consider the possibility of using less restrictive alternatives, such as postrelease supervision, halfway houses, or other methods.... This Court has said that a failure to consider, or to use, "alternative and less harsh methods" to achieve a nonpunitive objective can help to show that legislature's "purpose was to punish." And one can draw a similar conclusion here. Legislation that seeks to help the individual offender as well as to protect the public would avoid significantly greater restriction of an individual's liberty than public safety requires....

Thus, the practical experiences of other States, as revealed by other statutes, confirms what the Kansas Supreme Court's finding, the timing of the civil commitment proceeding, and the failure to consider less restrictive alternatives, themselves suggest, namely, that for Ex Post Facto Clause purposes, the purpose of the Kansas Act (as applied to previously convicted offenders) has a punitive, rather than a purely civil, purpose.

Source: *Kansas v. Hendricks*, 521 U.S. 346, 383–389 (1997) (J. Breyer, dissenting).

of the legislative supporters of the law saw it as a way to continue to detain dangerous sex offenders for whom effective treatment was impossible. These legislators simply saw the law as a way to increase the criminal sentences of these convicted sex offenders. Breyer noted that state officials did not seek to provide treatment to sex offenders when they first went to prison, but only "after they have served virtually their entire criminal sentence."[85]

Convicted sex offenders should go to jail for the criminal offenses they commit after a trial that affords the full protections of due process. These offenders should not, however, be indefinitely confined before they commit another crime. The *New York Times* in a 2006 editorial explained that the treatment rationale for civil confinement laws is mere pretense. "Sexual compulsions are notoriously difficult to treat, and the fact that virtually nobody successfully completes treatment programs strongly suggests that this particular justification for civil confinement programs is a sham."[86]

Civil confinement of sex offenders after incarceration violates constitutional rights.

The confinement of sex offenders after their incarceration is a form of punishment—a form of double punishment that violates the constitutional prohibition against double jeopardy. The central purpose of the double jeopardy clause is to prohibit the government from imposing or simply seeking a second punishment when it is not happy with the first punishment. That is essentially what civil confinement laws do when they are applied to a person who has completed his criminal sentence. The National Association of Criminal Defense Lawyers made this point in its amicus brief in the *Kansas v. Hendricks* case, adding: "While the State of Kansas is undoubtedly entitled to crack down on those it has not yet punished, it cannot add to the penalty it previously imposed on Mr. Hendricks, because that would violate the Double Jeopardy Clause."[87]

If one believes that sex offenders should stay in prison longer, that argument should be presented to the state legislature for an amending of state sentencing laws. Society should not subvert the Constitution in order to appeal to public pressure. Justice Anthony Kennedy was the tiebreaker in *Hendricks* when the Supreme Court upheld the constitutionality of Kansas's civil confinement law by a 5 to 4 vote. Kennedy wrote a separate concurring opinion, warning at the end: "If, however, civil confinement were to become a mechanism for retribution or general deterrence, or if it were shown that mental abnormality is too imprecise a category to offer a solid basis for concluding that civil detention is justified, our precedents would not suffice to validate it."[88]

THE LETTER OF THE LAW

South Carolina Statute on Civil Confinement of Sex Offenders

§ 44–48–120. Petition of release; hearing ordered by court.

If the Director of the Department of Mental Health determines that the person's mental abnormality or personality disorder has so changed that the person is safe to be at large and, if released, is not likely to commit acts of sexual violence, the director must authorize the person to petition the court for release. The petition must be served upon the court and the Attorney General. The Attorney General must notify the victim of the proceeding. The court, upon receipt of the petition for release, must order a hearing within 30 days. The Attorney General must represent the State and has the right to have the petitioner examined by experts chosen by the State. The hearing must be before a jury if requested by either the petitioner or the Attorney General. The burden of proof is upon the Attorney General to show beyond a reasonable doubt that the petitioner's mental abnormality or personality disorder remains such that the petitioner is not safe to be at large and, that if released, is likely to commit acts of sexual violence.

Source: S.C. Code Ann. § 44–48–120 (2007).

Less restrictive alternatives and procedural protections are needed to prevent indefinite confinement.

A basic staple of jurisprudence in the United States is that a prisoner is released after he has served his sentence. The individual has paid his debt to society. The mind-set among many state legislators, however, appears to be to find a way to simply lock away sex offenders and throw away the key, even after the offenders have served their criminal sentences.

About 20 states have passed these civil commitment laws, many of which do not provide proper treatment or consider less restrictive alternatives. One proposed alternative includes court-ordered treatment without complete confinement.[89] Another feature that needs to be implemented is an individualized treatment plan that focuses on the specific needs and problems of the offender. There is also a need for more reevaluations to determine whether an individual remains a danger and whether treatment is working.

For example, South Carolina's law provides that, if the director of mental health determines that the sex offender's status or condition has improved enough that he or she is no longer likely to commit future acts of sexual violence, the state attorney general must provide a hearing for the person. At that hearing, the attorney general must prove beyond a reasonable doubt—a very high standard used in criminal cases—that the offender's disorder is still present and he or she remains a danger.[90]

The civil commitment of sex offenders harms or takes away resources for other problems.

It costs states a significant amount of money to confine sexually violent predators indefinitely in "civil" institutions. It costs more than housing prison inmates, and also takes precious resources away from the treatment of those with mental illnesses.

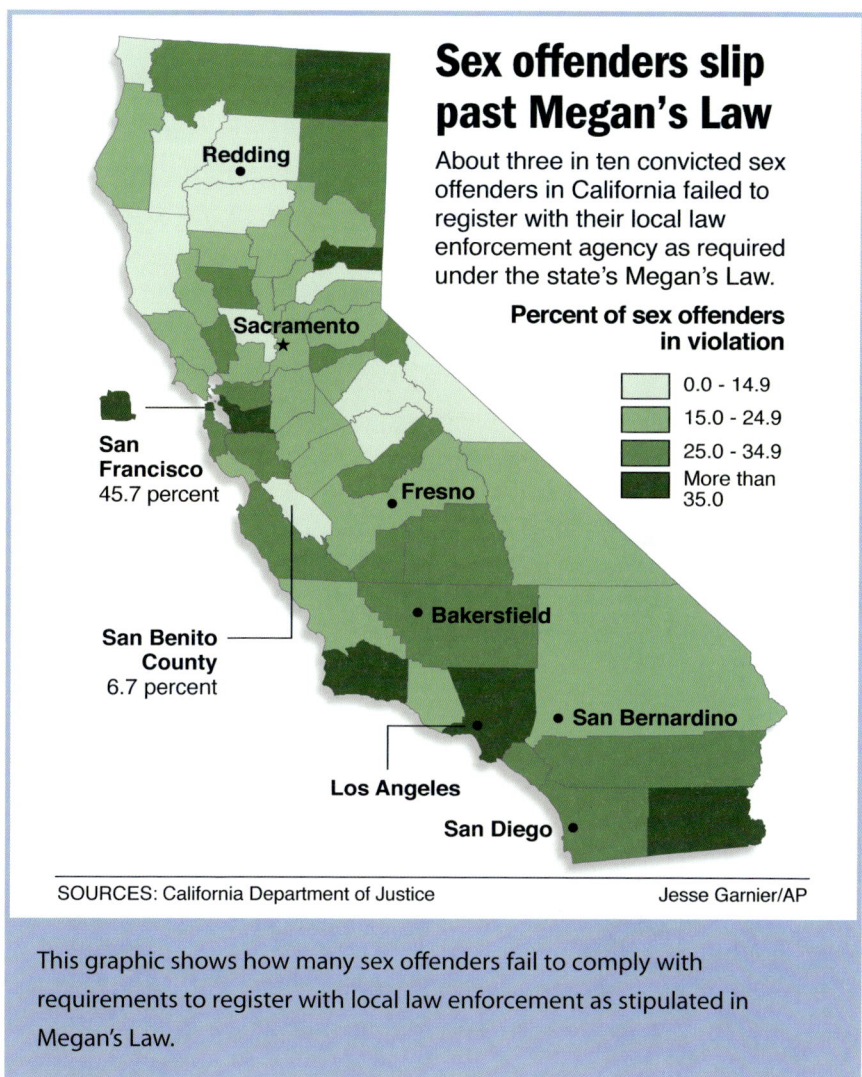

This graphic shows how many sex offenders fail to comply with requirements to register with local law enforcement as stipulated in Megan's Law.

Summary

The civil confinement of sex offenders after incarceration is punitive. Labeling the confinement as "civil" belies its criminal nature. Civil commitment of sex offenders after incarceration

Taking a Stand: Position of the National Association of State Mental Health Program Directors

The Court's conclusion that the civil commitment of dangerous sex offenders who do not have a mental illness is constitutional does not necessarily mean that such laws represent good policy. The National Association of State Mental Health Program Directors (NASMHPD) believes that some statutes could have severe and negative consequences for people with mental illnesses and for the public mental health system.

Specifically, NASMHPD believes that legislation allowing for the civil commitment of dangerous sex offenders who do not have a mental illness to psychiatric hospitals following completion of their prison sentences creates the following significant risks:

Laws which provide for the civil commitment of dangerous sex offenders for purposes that are principally punitive or for the purpose of continuing confinement, rather than for the purpose of providing treatment or psychiatric services, disrupt the state's ability to provide services for people with treatable psychiatric illnesses and undermine the mission and integrity of the public mental health system.

The civil commitment of dangerous sex offenders who may or may not respond to existing treatment modalities and who will require enormous resources for very long lengths of stay diverts scarce resources away from people who have been diagnosed with a mental illness and who both need and desire treatment.

The commitment of dangerous sex offenders to psychiatric facilities could endanger the safety of others in those facilities who have treatable psychiatric illnesses.

Source: National Association of State Mental Health Program Directors, "Position Statement on Laws Providing for the Civil Commitment of Sexually Violent Criminal Offenders," available online at http://www.nasmhpd.org/general_files/position_statement/sexpred.htm.

is a double form of punishment akin to double jeopardy. These deprivations of liberty also violate the ex post facto clause because they make something a crime when it was not previously. In fact, these statutes punish someone for their status,

QUOTABLE

Author Michelle L. Meloy

Because of ethical concerns, the potential for misuse and abuse of civil commitment statutes, and the drain on resources for preventative detention to both the criminal justice system and forensic mental health systems, it is evident that civil commitment statutes not be the policy of choice to deal with high-risk sex offenders. Rather, a more prudent policy is to encourage and systematically support conventional criminal sanctions to be used properly.

Source: Michelle L. Meloy, *Sex Offenses and the Men Who Commit Them: An Assessment of Sex Offenders on Probation*. Boston: Northeastern University Press, 2006, p. 51.

rather than for a criminal act. In essence, these laws punish someone because society thinks he or she will commit a crime in the future. Legal commentator Edward Ra wrote: "It is critical that states properly balance society's interest in protecting the public with the fundamental liberty and fairness interests of those whom the state is seeking to confine."[91] These laws do not strike the proper balance.

Legislatures should consider less restrictive alternatives, such as better treatment of these individuals in a less than totally confined setting. Perhaps there could be additional parole conditions placed on the individuals. At the very least, these statutes should be used only with a very narrow class of offenders and should employ strict procedural protections, such as regular review or reevaluations of the person's condition. Otherwise, society will be sacrificing constitutional principles of fundamental fairness for political expediency.

CONCLUSION

Unanswered Questions and the Future of Sex Offender Legislation

The problem of sex offenders and what to do with them will continue to be debated in the future. More studies are needed to establish whether existing sex crime laws are effective at reducing child abuse. Further studies need to be done to determine the recidivism rate of sex offenders and whether treatment of sex offenders can be effective. As author Michelle Meloy writes in her book *Sex Offenses and the Men Who Commit Them: An Assessment of Sex Offenders on Probation*, "The more that is understood about the risks associated with sexual offending and sexual victimization, the more that can be done to prevent it."[92] She goes on to warn that, so far, "researchers are unable to provide a clear, definitive answer regarding the true extent of recidivism."[93]

Any time a child is abused or murdered, there are renewed clarion calls for more advanced legislation. Three common restrictions on sex offenders are registration and notification laws, residency restrictions, and civil commitment laws. Congress continues to amend these various types of laws, and more and more states are passing new legislation.

Other alternatives might come in the future. Findlaw.com legal commentator Julie Hilden persuasively writes, for example, that judges in the future might establish pedophile-free zones (another name for residential restrictions) as a condition of probation for certain offenders. She writes that constitutional challenges to such measures would likely fail: "The far more oppressive punishment of prison is constitutional. Also, the significantly more oppressive punishment of home arrest can be constitutionally imposed as a condition of probation. So, then, how can it be that staying away from pedophile-free zones around bus stops, schools, parks, and playgrounds cannot be imposed as a condition of probation?"[94]

Law professor Marci Hamilton warns that existing measures, such as the 2006 Adam Walsh Act, do not go far enough to protect children. She believes that the existing databases of convicted sex offenders don't nearly cover the gamut of these offenders. "Parents also need to remember that the database will not be a truly comprehensive list of predators," she writes. "It will not have every adult accused of child abuse, because it includes only criminal convictions, not successful civil lawsuits."[95]

These are by no means the only types of measures being debated in legislative and political circles. Mandatory DNA testing of sex offenders, chemical castration, GPS tracking and monitoring, and more intensive methods of treatment continue to be discussed and debated.

On the legislative front, Congress has been very active. One measure examines how to deal with the problem of sex offenders on an international scale. In April 2008, several members of the House of Representatives introduced the International Megan's Law of 2008, H.R. 5722. This proposed measure would provide for online dissemination of information about sex offenders

Proposed Law: International Megan's Law of 2008

(a) Findings: Congress finds the following:

(1) Megan Nicole Kanka, who was 7 years old, was abducted, sexually assaulted, and murdered in 1994, in the State of New Jersey by a violent predator who had been convicted previously of a sex offense.

(2) In 1996, Congress adopted Megan's Law (Public Law 104–145) as a means to encourage States to inform the public of sex offenders who had been convicted and are present in their communities.

(3) In 2006, Congress adopted the Sex Offender Registration and Notification Act (title I of Public Law 109–248), which further strengthens the national standards for sex offender registration and public notification.

(4) Since 2003, U.S. Immigration and Customs Enforcement has made nearly 11,000 arrests, including over 9,100 arrests of non-United States citizens, of persons suspected of illegally exploiting children. Violations include child pornography, child sex tourism and facilitators, and trafficking of minors.

(5) It is estimated that more than 2 million children are exploited each year in the global commercial sex trade.

(b) Declaration of Purposes: The purposes of this Act and the amendments made by this Act are to prevent the international travel of sex traffickers and other sex offenders who intend to commit a sexual offense by—

(1) expanding access to information about known sex offenders in the United States who intend to travel outside the United States;

(2) ensuring that foreign nationals who have committed a sex offense are denied entry into the United States;

(3) including information in the annual report to Congress required by section 110(b)(1) of the Trafficking Victims Protection Act of 2000 (22 U.S.C. 7107(b)(1)) regarding the establishment of systems to identify and provide notice of international travel by sex offenders to destination countries; and

(4) providing assistance to foreign countries under the Foreign Assistance Act of 1961 to meet the requirements described in paragraph (3).

Source: H.R. 5722 (2008).

who travel internationally—both convicted sex offenders leaving the United States to other countries and convicted sex offenders from other countries seeking to enter the United States. This measure recognizes that sexual abuse and sexual victimization is much more than a national problem; it is an international problem. Particularly in the age of the Internet, legislators, law enforcement officials, and others need to be aware that harm also comes from farther away than a few thousand feet from a school.

Other measures introduced in Congress include a measure that would eliminate parole for those convicted of sexual abuse of minors,[96] create a separate database of the DNA of child sexual predators,[97] and create more funding for more personnel to enforce child pornography and obscenity laws.[98]

From the FBI: Dangers to Children from Online Predators

While on-line computer exploration opens a world of possibilities for children, expanding their horizons and exposing them to different cultures and ways of life, they can be exposed to dangers as they hit the road exploring the information highway. There are individuals who attempt to sexually exploit children through the use of on-line services and the Internet. Some of these individuals gradually seduce their targets through the use of attention, affection, kindness, and even gifts. These individuals are often willing to devote considerable amounts of time, money, and energy in this process. They listen to and empathize with the problems of children. They will be aware of the latest music, hobbies, and interests of children. These individuals attempt to gradually lower children's inhibitions by slowly introducing sexual context and content into their conversations.

Source: Federal Bureau of Investigation, "A Parent's Guide to Internet Safety," available online at http://www.fbi.gov/publications/pguide/parentsguide.pdf.

Another area that lawmakers will address is the problem of sexual solicitations of children by adults over the Internet. In fiscal year 2007, the FBI opened up 2,400 new cases involving online predators.[99] Numerous children have been enticed into sexual encounters with adults posing as children over the Internet. One measure recently introduced in Congress would prohibit sex offenders from accessing social networking sites, such as MySpace, to contact minors.[100]

The courts are now dealing with numerous constitutional challenges to the Adam Walsh Act. The ultimate outcome of those challenges could impact other proposed measures dealing with sex offenders.

No one doubts that the protection of children should remain a paramount governmental interest in the future. The protection of minors and other victims of sexual abuse is compelling. At the same time, the rush to protect minors and other sexual abuse victims must be balanced against basic constitutional principles. Some people—including many who study these issues for a living—fervently believe that at least some of the legislation in recent years goes too far, trampling on the rights of sex offenders and infringing on fundamental constitutional freedoms. That will be the great task for society in the foreseeable future: balancing liberty versus security in an increasingly complex, mobile, and at times dangerous world.

APPENDIX

Beginning Legal Research

The goals of each book in the POINT/COUNTERPOINT series are not only to give the reader a basic introduction to a controversial issue affecting society, but also to encourage the reader to explore the issue more fully. This Appendix is meant to serve as a guide to the reader in researching the current state of the law as well as exploring some of the public policy arguments as to why existing laws should be changed or new laws are needed.

Although some sources of law can be found primarily in law libraries, legal research has become much faster and more accessible with the advent of the Internet. This Appendix discusses some of the best starting points for free access to laws and court decisions, but surfing the Web will uncover endless additional sources of information. Before you can research the law, however, you must have a basic understanding of the American legal system.

The most important source of law in the United States is the Constitution. Originally enacted in 1787, the Constitution outlines the structure of our federal government, as well as setting limits on the types of laws that the federal government and state governments can enact. Through the centuries, a number of amendments have added to or changed the Constitution, most notably the first 10 amendments, which collectively are known as the "Bill of Rights" and which guarantee important civil liberties.

Reading the plain text of the Constitution provides little information. For example, the Constitution prohibits "unreasonable searches and seizures" by the police. To understand concepts in the Constitution, it is necessary to look to the decisions of the U.S. Supreme Court, which has the ultimate authority in interpreting the meaning of the Constitution. For example, the U.S. Supreme Court's 2001 decision in *Kyllo v. United States* held that scanning the outside of a person's house using a heat sensor to determine whether the person is growing marijuana is an unreasonable search—if it is done without first getting a search warrant from a judge. Each state also has its own constitution and a supreme court that is the ultimate authority on its meaning.

Also important are the written laws, or "statutes," passed by the U.S. Congress and the individual state legislatures. As with constitutional provisions, the U.S. Supreme Court and the state supreme courts are the ultimate authorities in interpreting the meaning of federal and state laws, respectively. However, the U.S. Supreme Court might find that a state law violates the U.S. Constitution, and a state supreme court might find that a state law violates either the state or U.S. Constitution.

APPENDIX

Not every controversy reaches either the U.S. Supreme Court or the state supreme courts, however. Therefore, the decisions of other courts are also important. Trial courts hear evidence from both sides and make a decision, while appeals courts review the decisions made by trial courts. Sometimes rulings from appeals courts are appealed further to the U.S. Supreme Court or the state supreme courts.

Lawyers and courts refer to statutes and court decisions through a formal system of citations. Use of these citations reveals which court made the decision or which legislature passed the statute, and allows one to quickly locate the statute or court case online or in a law library. For example, the Supreme Court case *Brown v. Board of Education* has the legal citation 347 U.S. 483 (1954). At a law library, this 1954 decision can be found on page 483 of volume 347 of the U.S. Reports, which are the official collection of the Supreme Court's decisions. On the following page, you will find sample of all the major kinds of legal citation.

Finding sources of legal information on the Internet is relatively simple thanks to "portal" sites such as findlaw.com and lexisone.com, which allow the user to access a variety of constitutions, statutes, court opinions, law review articles, news articles, and other useful sources of information. For example, findlaw.com offers access to all Supreme Court decisions since 1893. Other useful sources of information include gpo.gov, which contains a complete copy of the U.S. Code, and thomas.loc.gov, which offers access to bills pending before Congress, as well as recently passed laws. Of course, the Internet changes every second of every day, so it is best to do some independent searching.

Of course, many people still do their research at law libraries, some of which are open to the public. For example, some state governments and universities offer the public access to their law collections. Law librarians can be of great assistance, as even experienced attorneys need help with legal research from time to time.

Common Citation Forms

Source of Law	Sample Citation	Notes
U.S. Supreme Court	*Employment Division v. Smith*, 485 U.S. 660 (1988)	The U.S. Reports is the official record of Supreme Court decisions. There is also an unofficial Supreme Court ("S. Ct.") reporter.
U.S. Court of Appeals	*United States v. Lambert*, 695 F.2d 536 (11th Cir. 1983)	Appellate cases appear in the Federal Reporter, designated by "F." The 11th Circuit has jurisdiction in Alabama, Florida, and Georgia.
U.S. District Court	*Carillon Importers, Ltd. v. Frank Pesce Group, Inc.*, 913 F.Supp. 1559 (S.D.Fla. 1996)	Federal trial-level decisions are reported in the Federal Supplement ("F. Supp."). Some states have multiple federal districts; this case originated in the Southern District of Florida.
U.S. Code	Thomas Jefferson Commemoration Commission Act, 36 U.S.C., §149 (2002)	Sometimes the popular names of legislation—names with which the public may be familiar—are included with the U.S. Code citation.
State Supreme Court	*Sterling v. Cupp*, 290 Ore. 611, 614, 625 P.2d 123, 126 (1981)	The Oregon Supreme Court decision is reported in both the state's reporter and the Pacific regional reporter.
State Statute	Pennsylvania Abortion Control Act of 1982, 18 Pa. Cons. Stat. 3203-3220 (1990)	States use many different citation formats for their statutes.

Cases

***Allen v. Illinois,* 478 U.S. 364 (1968)**
In this decision, the U.S. Supreme Court ruled that a defendant did not have a Fifth Amendment privilege against self-incrimination in a civil proceeding to determine whether he was a sexually dangerous person under an Illinois law. The defendant had argued that he did not have a Fifth Amendment right not to testify in these "criminal" proceedings. The Court ruled 5 to 4 that the proceedings were civil and that the constitutional right did not attach.

***Connecticut Department of Public Safety v. Doe,* 538 U.S. 1 (2003)**
In this decision, the U.S. Supreme Court ruled that a Connecticut sex offender notification law that provided much information about sex offenders to the public via an online registry did not violate the due-process rights of convicted sex offenders.

***Doe v. Miller,* 405 F.3d 700 (8th Cir. 2005)**
In this decision, a divided 8th U.S. Circuit Court of Appeals upheld Iowa's 2,000-foot residential restriction on convicted sex offenders.

***Kansas v. Hendricks,* 521 U.S. 346 (1997)**
In this decision, the U.S. Supreme Court upheld 5 to 4 a Kansas law that allowed the state to impose civil confinement on sexually violent predators. The defendant had argued that the law violated double jeopardy under the Fifth Amendment and also constituted an impermissible ex post facto law. The court ruled that the law was not punitive in purpose and was a civil, not a criminal, law.

***People v. Cornelius,* 821 N.E.2d 288 (Ill. 2004)**
In this decision, the Illinois Supreme Court upheld the state's Megan's Law. It rejected challenges that the Megan's Law violated rights to privacy, due process, and equal protection.

***Seling v. Young,* 531 U.S. 250 (2001)**
In this decision, the U.S. Supreme Court upheld a Washington law that provided for the civil confinement of certain sex offenders.

***Smith v. Doe,* 538 U.S 84 (2003)**
In this decision, the U.S. Supreme Court ruled that an Alaska law requiring registration by sex offenders and public notification of certain information did not violate the ex post facto clause of the Constitution.

***Weems v. Little Rock Police Department,* 453 F.3d 1010 (8th Cir. 2006)**
In this decision, the 8th U.S. Circuit Court of Appeals rejected constitutional challenges to a state law restricting the residency of sex offenders.

Terms and Concepts

Adam's Law
amicus brief

ELEMENTS OF THE ARGUMENT

double jeopardy
due process
equal protection
ex post facto
fundamental right
Jessica's Law
Megan's Law
online sex offender registry
rational basis
recidivism
strict scrutiny

NOTES

Introduction: The Sex Offender Problem

1 Anne-Marie McAlinden, *The Shaming of Sexual Offenders: Risk, Retribution and Reintegration* (Portland, OR: Hart Publishing, 2007), 3.
2 *McLune v. Lile*, 536 U.S. 24, 33 (2002).
3 Tennessee Sexual Offender Registry. Available online at http://www.ticic.state.tn.us/sorinternet/sosearch.aspx.
4 Seamus McGraw. "Suffer the Children: The Story of Megan's Law." Available online at http://www.crimelibrary.com/serial_killers/predators/kanka/1.html.
5 *State v. Pollard*, (No. 05A02-0707-CR-640)(Ind.App.)(5/13/2008).

Point: Registration and Notification Requirements for Convicted Sex Offenders Are Constitutional

6 Megan Nicole Kanka Foundation. Available online at http://www.megannicolekankafoundation.org/mission.htm.
7 *Ibid.*
8 Federal Megan's Law. Available online at http://www.megannicolekankafoundation.org/federal_law.htm.
9 *Smith v. Doe*, 538 U.S. 84 (2003).
10 *Connecticut Dept. of Public Safety v. Doe*, 538 U.S. 1 (2003).
11 *Smith v. Doe*, 98.
12 *Connecticut Dept. of Public Safety v. Doe*, 7.
13 *Ibid.*
14 *People v. Cornelius*, 821 N.E.2d 288 (Il. 2004).
15 *Ibid.*, 299.
16 *Ibid.*, 300.
17 Crimes Against Children Research Center. "New Data Show Child Sexual Abuse Down 5% Nationally," April 16, 2008. Available online at http://www.unh.edu/news/cj_nr/2008/April/lw16data.cfm.
18 Brian J. Telpner, "Constructing Safe Communities: Megan's Laws and the Purposes of Punishment," *Georgetown Law Journal* 85 (1997): 2039.

Counterpoint: Registration and Notification Laws Are Unconstitutional

19 Jon Nordheimer, "'Vigilante' Attack in New Jersey Is Linked to Sex-Offenders Law," *New York Times*, January 11, 1995, A1.
20 *Ibid.*
21 Maria Newman, "Paroled Rapist Says He's the Victim Now: Target of Gunman Contends 'Megan's Law Has Stolen His Freedom,'" *New York Times*, November 14, 1998, B1.
22 Janny Scott, "Sex Offender Due for Parole, But No Place Will Have Him," *New York Times*, September 19, 1994, A1.
23 Rachel King, "Sex Offender Registries: Public Safety or Public Hazard?" *Oldspeak*, May 18, 2006. Available online at http://www.rutherford.org/Oldspeak/Articles/Law/oldspeak-sexregistries.asp.
24 Patty Wetterling, "The harm in sex-offender laws," *Sacramento Bee*, September 14, 2007. Available online at http://www.sacbee.com/110/v-print/story/377462.html.
25 *Ibid.*
26 Sarah Tofte, "Protect children from sexual violence," *San Gabriel Valley Tribune*, January 21, 2008.
27 Human Rights Watch. "No Easy Answers: Sex Offender Laws in the United States." September 2007. Available online at http://www.hrw.org/reports/2007/us0907/index.htm.
28 Human Rights Watch, "No Easy Answers."
29 King, "Sex Offender Registries."
30 Bureau of Justice Statistics. "5 Percent of Sex Offenders Rearrested for Another Sex Crime Within 3 Years of Prison Release," U.S. Department of Justice, Office of Justice Programs, November 16, 2003. Available online at http://www.ojp.gov/bjs/pub/press/rsorp94pr.htm.
31 Human Rights Watch, "No Easy Answers."
32 McAlinden, *The Shaming of Sexual Offenders*, 79.
33 Michelle L. Meloy. *Sex Offenses and the Men Who Commit Them: An Assessment of Sex Offenders on Probation.* Boston: Northeastern University Press, 2006, 11.

NOTES

Point: Residency Restrictions Are a Constitutional Way to Protect Victims from Sex Offenders
34 *Doe v. Miller*, 405 F.3d 700, 707 (8th Cir. 2005).
35 *Ibid.*
36 *Ibid.*, 719.
37 *Ibid.*, 722.
38 *Weems v. Little Rock Police Department*, 453 F.3d 1010 (8th Cir. 2006).
39 *Ibid.*, 1014.
40 *Ibid.*, 1018.
41 *People v. Leroy*, 828 N.E.2d 769 (Ill.App. 2005).
42 *Ibid.*, 777.
43 David Yepsen, "Law makes life difficult for sex offenders? Too bad," *Des Moines Register*, October 18, 2005, 18A.

Counterpoint: Residency Restrictions Against Sexual Offenders Violate Constitutional Rights
44 Human Rights Watch, "No Easy Answers."
45 Wendy Koch, "Sex-offender residency laws get second look," *USA Today*, February 26, 2007. Available online at http://www.usatoday.com/news/nation/2007-02-25-sex-offender-laws-cover_x.htm.
46 Julie Hilden. "Are Pedophile-Free Zones Constitutional? The Issues That They Raise," Findlaw.com. August 30, 2005. Available online at http://writ.news.findlaw.com/scripts/printer_friendly.pl?page=hilden/20050830.html.
47 Koch, "Sex-offender residency laws get second look."
48 Human Rights Watch, "No Easy Answers."
49 Quoted in Catherine Elton, "Behind the Picket Fence," *Boston Globe*, May 6, 2007, 34.
50 Minnesota Department of Corrections. "Residential Proximity & Sex Offense Recidivism in Minnesota." Available online at http://theparson.net/so/04-07MinnesotaSexOffenderReport-Proximity.pdf.
51 Iowa County Attorneys Association. "Statement of Sex Offender Residency Restrictions in Iowa," February 14, 2006. Available online at http://www.cacj.org/PDF/2006/Statement%20on%20Sex%20Offender%20Residency%20Restrictions.pdf.
52 *Ibid.*
53 *Mann v. Georgia Dept. of Corrections* (No. SO7A1043) (Ga.) (11/21/2007).
54 *Ibid.*
55 *Ibid.*
56 405 F.3d 700 (8th Cir. 2005).
57 *Ibid.*, 724 (J. Mellow, concurring in part and dissenting in part).
58 *Indiana v. Pollard*, No. 05A02–0707-CR-640 (Ind.App., 5/13/2008).
59 *Ibid.*, 10.
60 *Ibid.*, 11.
61 Meghan Sil Towers, "Protectionism, Punishment and Pariahs: Sex Offenders and Residence Restrictions," *Journal of Law & Policy* 15 (2007): 291.
62 Human Rights Watch, "No Easy Answers."

Point: Civil Commitment of Violent Sexual Predators Is Necessary and Constitutional
63 Roxanne Lieb. "Washington's Sexually Violent Predator Law: Legislative History and Comparison with Other States," Washington State Institute for Public Policy, December 1996. Available online at http://www.wsipp.wa.gov/rptfiles/WAsexlaw.pdf.
64 *Kansas v. Hendricks*, 521 U.S. 346 (1997).
65 *Ibid.*, 354–355.
66 *Ibid.*, 357.
67 *Jacobson v. Massachusetts*, 197 U.S. 11, 26 (1905).
68 309 U.S. 270 (1940).
69 *Addington v. Texas*, 441 U.S. 418, 426 (1979).
70 509 U.S. 312 (1993).
71 *Hendricks*, 521 U.S., 362.
72 *Ibid.*
73 *Ibid.*
74 *Ibid.*, 363.
75 *Ibid.*, 364.
76 *Ibid.*, 370.
77 *Seling v. Young*, 531 U.S. 250 (2001).
78 *Kansas v. Crane*, 534 U.S. 407 (2002)
79 *Ibid.*, 412.
80 Edward P. Ra, "The Civil Confinement of Sexual Predators: A Delicate Balance," *St. John's Journal of Legal Commentary* 23 (2007): 335.

Counterpoint: Civil Commitment Proceedings Are Punitive and Violate Constitutional Rights

81 Richard G. Wright, "Parole and Probation: Sex Offender Post-Incarceration Sanctions: Are There Any Limits?" *New England Journal on Criminal and Civil Confinement* 34 (2008): 17.
82 Abby Goodnough and Monica Davey, "A Record of Failure at Center for Sex Offenders," *New York Times*, March 5, 2007. Available online at http://www.nytimes.com/2007/03/05/us/05civil.html?pagewanted=1&_r=1.
83 *Kansas v. Hendricks*, 521 U.S. 346 (1997).
84 Monica Davey and Abby Goodnough, "Doubts Rise as States Hold Sex Offenders After Prison," *New York Times*, March 4, 2007. Available online at http://www.nytimes.com/2007/03/04/us/04civil.html?_r=1&pagewanted=print&oref=slogin.
85 *Kansas v. Hendricks* (J. Breyer, dissenting).
86 "Rush to Judgment on Sex Offenders," *New York Times*, December 10, 2006, 15.
87 Amicus Brief of the National Association of Criminal Defense Lawyers and the Kansas Association of Criminal Defense Lawyers, *Kansas v. Hendricks*, August 16, 1996, 45.
88 *Kansas v. Hendricks*, 521 U.S. 346, 373 (J. Kennedy, concurring).
89 Ra, "The Civil Confinement of Sexual Predators," 335, 367.
90 S.C. Ann. § 44–48–120.
91 Ra, "The Civil Confinement of Sexual Predators," 335, 364.

Conclusion: Unanswered Questions and the Future of Sex Offender Legislation

92 Meloy, *Sex Offenses and the Men Who Commit Them*, 2.
93 *Ibid.*, 19.
94 Hilden, "Are Pedophile-Free Zones Constitutional?"
95 Marci Hamilton. "Congress Passes the 'Adam Walsh Bill' to Protect Children from Abuse: It Is a Good Start, But More Needs to Be Done to Make It Effective," Findlaw Writ, July 27, 2006. Available online at http://writ.news.findlaw.com/hamilton/20060727.html.
96 No Parole of Sex Offenders Act, H.R. 2016, introduced May 21, 2007.
97 Save Our Children: Stop the Violent Predators Against Children Act of 2007, H.R. 252 (2007).
98 Combating Child Exploitation Act of 2007, S. 1738 (2007).
99 Alberto R. Gonzalez, "Target sexual predators: We owe it to our children to protect them. New, tougher laws would help to do that," *USA Today*, May 14, 2008, 11A.
100 Sex Offender Internet Prohibition Act of 2007, H.R. 3144.

RESOURCES

Books and Articles

Bureau of Justice Statistics. "Recidivism of Sex Offenders Released from Prison in 1994." November 2003. Available online. URL: http://www.ojp.usdoj.gov/bjs/pub/pdf/rsorp94.pdf. Accessed June 20, 2008.

Durling, Caleb. "Never going home: does it make us safer? Does it make sense? Sex offenders, residency restrictions, and reforming risk management law." *Journal of Criminal Law & Criminology* 97, no. 1 (2006): 317.

George, Shelley. "Slipping Through the Cracks and Into Schools: The Need for a Uniform Sexual-Predator Tracking System." *SCHOLAR* 10, no. 2 (2008): 117.

Goldstein, Debra H., and Stephanie Goldstein. "Sex Offender Registration & Notification: The Constitution vs. Public Safety." *Alabama Lawyer* 60 (1999): 112.

Greenfield, Lawrence. "Sex Offenses & Offenders: An Analysis of Data on Rape and Sexual Assault." U.S. Department of Justice, 1997. Available online. URL: http://www.ojp.usdoj.gov/bjs/pdf/soo.pdf. Accessed June 20, 2008.

Hanson, R. Karl. "Recidivism and Age: Follow-Up Data from 4,673 Sex Offenders," *Journal of Interpersonal Violence* 17, no. 10 (2002): 1046–1062.

Human Rights Watch. "No Easy Answers: Sex Offender Laws in the United States." September 2007. Available online. URL: http://www.hrw.org/reports/2007/us0907/index.htm. Accessed June 20, 2008.

La Fond, John Q. "The Costs of Enacting a Sexual Predator Law." *Psychology Public Policy & Law* 4 (1998): 468.

Logan, Wayne A. *Knowledge as Power: A History of Criminal Registration Laws in America.* Palo Alto, Calif: Stanford University Press, 2009.

McAlinden, Anne-Marie. *The Shaming of Sexual Offenders: Risk, Retribution and Reintegration.* Portland, Ore.: Hart Publishing, 2007.

Meloy, Michelle. *Sex Offenses and the Men Who Commit Them: An Assessment of Sex Offenders on Probation.* Boston: Northeastern University Press, 2006.

Minnesota Department of Corrections. "Residential Proximity & Sex Offense Recidivism in Minnesota." April 2007. Available online. URL:

RESOURCES

http://theparson.net/so/04–07MinnesotaSexOffenderReport-Proximity.pdf. Accessed June 20, 2008.

Morse, Stephen J. "Blame and Danger: An Essay on Preventative Detention." *Boston University Law Review* 76, no. 1/2 (1996): 113.

Ra, Edward P. "The Civil Confinement of Sexual Predators: A Delicate Balance." *St. John's Journal of Legal Commentary* 22 (2007): 335, 364.

Sample, Lisa L. "An Examination of the Degree to Which Sex Offenders Kill." *Criminal Justice Policy Review* 31 (2006): 230.

Sample, Lisa L., and Timothy W. Bray. "Are Sex Offenders Different? An Examination of Re-arrest Patterns." *Criminal Justice Policy Review* 17 (2006): 83.

Singleton, David A. "Sex Offender Registry Statutes and the Culture of Beer: The Case for More Meaningful Rational Basis Review of Fear." *Thomas Law Journal* 3 (2006): 600.

Telpner, Brian J. "Constructing Safe Communities: Megan's Laws and the Purposes of Punishment." *Georgetown Law Journal* 85 (1997): 2039.

Towers, Meghan Sil. "Protectionism, Punishment and Pariahs: Sex Offenders and Residence Restrictions." *Journal of Law and Policy* 15 (2007): 291.

Wright, Richard G. "Sex Offender Post Incarceration Sanctions: Are There Any Limits?" *New England Journal on Criminal and Civil Confinement* 34 (2008): 17.

Web Sites
Center for Sex Offender Management
http://www.csom.org

Crimes Against Children Research Center
http://www.unh.edu/ccrc

Family Watchdog
http://www.familywatchdog.us

Human Rights Watch
http://www.hrw.org

Megan Nicole Kanka Foundation
http://www.megannicolekankafoundation.org

RESOURCES

National Center for Missing and Exploited Children
http://www.missingkids.com

National Sex Offender Public Website
http://www.nsopr.gov

Parents for Megan's Law
http://www.parentsformeganslaw.com

Polly Klaas Foundation
http://www.pollyklaas.org

PICTURE CREDITS

PAGE

14: AP Images/Steve Helber
24: AP Images/Brian Branch Price
44: AP Images/Chris Kaeser
51: AP Images/Marci Stenberg
71: AP Images/Jesse Garnier

INDEX

A
Adam's law, 14, 16–17
Adam Walsh Child Protection and Safety Act (2006), 15, 22, 75, 78
Addington v. *Texas*, 59
Alabama
  residency restriction laws, 46
Alaska
  sex offender registration laws, 23–25, 28–30
Allison, Janet, 49
American Civil Liberties Union, 31
Arkansas
  residency restriction laws, 42–44, 46

B
Breyer, Stephen, 63, 67–68
Bureau of Justice Statistics, 36
Burger, Warren E., 59
Bush, George W.
  on signing Adam Walsh legislation, 16–17

C
chemical castration, 75
civil commitment
  laws, 75
  counterpoint, 65–73
  history, 58–61
  point, 56–64
  process of, 59
  requirements, 18–19, 56–64
Clinton, Bill, 22
Connecticut
  sex offender registration laws, 23, 25, 30

Connecticut Department of Public Safety v. *Doe*, 23
Constitution, United States
  challenges, 23–24, 26, 30, 60, 63, 75, 78
  double jeopardy, 61–64, 68
  ex post facto clause, 24–25, 53, 61, 63–64, 67, 71
  violations of, 18, 23–24, 31–38, 40, 48–50, 52–55, 61–73
Couey, John
  crimes, 15, 47
Crimes Against Children Research Center, 29, 50

D
Department of Public Safety's Web site, 28
deterrence, 62
Doe v. *Miller*
  and residency requirements, 41, 44, 53–54
Dru Sjodin National Sex Offender Public Web site, 15

F
federal laws
  Jacob's Law, 12, 14, 22, 33
  Megan's Law, 13–14, 22, 76
Finkelhor, David, 50
Florida
  civil commitment facilities, 65–66
  residency restriction laws, 46

Foreign Assistance Act (1961), 76

G
Georgia
  residency restriction laws, 52
  Supreme Court, 52–53
GPS tracking, 75

H
Hamilton, Marci, 75
Heller v. *Doe*, 60
Hendricks, Leroy
  crimes, 57–59, 61–63
  treatments, 66–67
Hilden, Julie, 49, 75
Howard University, 32, 35
Human Rights Watch, 34
  studies, 36–37, 48–49, 55

I
Illinois
  sex offender registration laws, 26–28, 46
  supreme court, 26–28
Indiana, 54
International Megan's Law (2008), 75–77
Internet Crimes Against Children Task Forces, 17
Iowa
  residency restriction laws, 39–41, 43–44, 47, 51, 54

J
Jacob's Law
  requirements of, 12, 22, 33
Jacob Wetterling Crimes Against Children Sex Offender Registration Act. *See* Jacob's Law

91

INDEX

Jessica's Laws
  electronic monitoring, 16
  minimum sentence, 11, 15–16

K
Kanka, Maureen, 21–22
Kanka, Megan Nicole
  crimes against, 12–13, 21, 30, 39, 47, 76
  parents, 13, 21–22
Kanka, Richard, 21–22
Kansas
  civil commitment laws, 57–58, 61–62, 67, 69
Kansas v. *Crane*, 63
Kansas v. *Hendricks*, 58, 66–69
Kennedy, Anthony, 25, 69
Kentucky
  civil commitment laws, 60
King, Rachel, 32, 35

L
law enforcement officials
  and notification legislation, 22, 27, 31
  protection of the public, 13, 17, 30, 50
legislation, sexual offenses
  civil commitment laws, 18–19, 75
  controversy, 18, 34–42, 49
  federal, 11–12
  future of, 74–78
  protection of children, 17, 30

registration and notification, 11–12, 18, 21–38, 42–43, 75
residency restrictions, 16–18, 39–55, 75
state, 11
Lunsford, Jessica
  crimes against, 15, 30, 39, 47

M
mandatory DNA testing, 75
  database, 77
Mann, Anthony, 52
Mann v. *Department of Corrections*, 52–53
McAlinden, Anne-Marie, 35
  The Shaming of Sexual Offenders: Risk, Retribution and Reintegration, 10
media
  demonizing sex offenders, 36–37
Megan's Laws
  critics of, 35–37
  keeping communities safer, 13, 22, 25, 28–29, 76
  federal version, 13–14
  and reduction of sexual offenses, 23–30, 35
  requirements, 22, 29, 32–33, 76
  state laws, 26, 30–31, 76
Melloy, Michael, 53–54
Meloy, Michelle, 35, 73
  Sex Offenses and the Men Who Commit Them: An Assessment of Sex Offenders on Probation, 74

mental illness, 70–71
  and sex offenders, 12, 18, 57, 59–60, 62–64, 69
Minnesota
  civil commitment laws, 59
  Department of Corrections, 50
Minnesota ex rel. Pearson v. *Probate Court of Ramsey Co.*, 59–60

N
National Association of Criminal Defense Lawyers, 68
National Association of State Mental Health Program Directors, 72
National Child Abuse Registry, 17, 22
National Sex Offender Registry, 16–17
New Jersey
  sex offender legislature, 22, 31, 76

O
Oklahoma
  residency restriction laws, 46

P
Pearson, Edwin, 59
pedophiles, 58
  free zones, 75
  and moral panic, 10, 34
People v. *Cornelius*, 26
People v. *Leroy*, 46
personality disorders
  and sexual offenders, 12, 57, 62

INDEX

public record
  criminal cases, 30
  notification, 12,
    14–15, 22–25,
    27, 38

R

Ra, Edward, 73
recidivism
  rates of, 11, 35–37, 50,
    64, 74
  and sexual offenses, 11,
    18, 25, 30, 35, 56
  studies on, 35–37
registration and notification laws, 75
  counterpoint, 31–38
  movement for, 12–14,
    16, 22
  national, 15
  online registries, 11,
    14–16, 25–28, 33, 49
  point, 21–30
  requirements, 11,
    14, 16, 26, 31–33,
    42–43, 45
residency restrictions, 75
  counterpoint, 48–55
  point, 39–47
  requirements, 16–18,
    39–47, 49
  research, 47, 50–52
retribution, 62
risk assessment process,
  45–46

S

Scarlet Letter-like
  punishment, 19, 24,
  33, 38, 48
Seling v. Young, 63
sex crimes, 10
  causes, 37
  child molestation,
    11, 18, 28, 37, 39,
    49, 74
  child prostitution and
    pornography, 16,
    76–77
  online predators, 77
  rape, 11, 31, 34, 48
  research and statistics,
    22–23, 74
  sex trafficking, 16
  sexual assault, 11
  sexual battery, 11
  solicitation of a minor,
    11, 17, 77–78
  trafficking of minors,
    76–77
Sex Offender Assessment
  Committee, 45
Sex Offender Registration
  Act (1997), 42–43, 76
sex offenders
  classes and differences,
    11, 15, 30, 34–35, 38,
    44, 46
  convictions, 10–12, 18,
    25–26, 30–33, 36,
    39–40, 43–46, 49, 59,
    61–64, 75
  institutionalize, 17,
    56–66, 70
  personality disorders, 12
  post-incarceration
    sanctions, 11, 14–19,
    23, 31, 38–73
  problem, 10–19, 21
  public notification, 11,
    14–15, 25–26
  and recidivism, 11, 18,
    25, 30, 35–37, 50, 56,
    64, 74
  research, 29, 32, 35–37
  rights of, 19, 23–29,
    32, 41–42, 52–55,
    65–73, 78
  treatments, 19, 34, 37,
    40, 47, 57, 63, 65–68,
    70–71, 75

*Sex Offenses and the Men
  Who Commit Them:
  An Assessment of Sex
  Offenders on Probation*
  (Meloy), 74
*Shaming of Sexual
  Offenders: Risk,
  Retribution and
  Reintegration, The*
  (McAlinden), 10
Shriner, Earl, 56
Smith v. Doe, 23, 25, 28
society
  dangers to, 10, 18,
    23, 28–30, 40, 56,
    58–59, 64
  debts to, 11, 18–19, 70
  dilemmas, 10, 15,
    24, 55, 65–66, 69,
    73, 78
South Carolina
  civil commitment laws,
    69–70
South Dakota
  residency restriction
    laws, 46
state laws, 15, 41
  civil commitment, 56
  Jessica's Laws, 11, 15
  Megan's Law, 13–14,
    22, 25–26, 29,
    31, 76
  residency restriction,
    39–55
Supreme Court
  justices, 25
  rulings, 24–25, 30,
    45–46, 57–64,
    66–67, 69

T

Telpner, Brian J., 29
Tennessee Sexual
  Offender Registry, 11
Thomas, Clarence, 59,
  61–63

INDEX

Timmendequas, Jesse
  crimes, 12–13, 21, 47
Tofte, Sarah, 33
Towers, Meghan Sil, 55
Trafficking Victims Protection Act (2000), 76

U

United States Congress
  legislation, 13–14, 15, 18, 22, 75–78

U.S. Immigration and Custom Enforcement, 76

V

vigilantism
  against registered sex offenders, 31–33, 38

W

Walsh, Adam
  crimes against, 14–15
  legislation, 14, 16–17
Walsh, John, 15
Walsh, Reve, 15
Washington
  civil commitment laws, 56, 58, 63
Weems v. *Little Rock Police Department*, 43
Wetterling, Jacob Erwin
  abduction, 12, 33
Wetterling, Patty, 33
Wright, Richard G., 65

CONTRIBUTORS

DAVID L. HUDSON JR., is an author-attorney who has published widely on First Amendment and other constitutional law issues. Hudson is a research attorney with the First Amendment Center at Vanderbilt University and a First Amendment contributing editor to the American Bar Association's *Preview of the United States Supreme Court Cases*. He obtained his undergraduate degree from Duke University and his law degree from Vanderbilt University Law School.

ALAN MARZILLI, M.A., J.D., lives in Birmingham, Alabama, and is a program associate with Advocates for Human Potential, Inc., a research and consulting firm based in Sudbury, Massachusetts, and Albany, New York. He primarily works on developing training and educational materials for agencies of the federal government on topics such as housing, mental health policy, employment, and transportation. He has spoken on mental health issues in 30 states, the District of Columbia, and Puerto Rico; his work has included training mental health administrators, nonprofit management and staff, and people with mental illnesses and their families on a wide variety of topics, including effective advocacy, community-based mental health services, and housing. He has written several handbooks and training curricula that are used nationally and as far away as the territory of Guam. He managed statewide and national mental health advocacy programs and worked for several public interest lobbying organizations while studying law at Georgetown University. He has written more than a dozen books, including numerous titles in the POINT/COUNTERPOINT series.